Sigrid Estrada

Nick Hornby is the author of the bestselling novels *Juliet, Naked, Slam, A Long Way Down, How to Be Good, High Fidelity,* and *About a Boy,* and the memoir *Fever Pitch*. He is also the author of *Songbook,* a finalist for a National Book Critics Circle Award, *Shakespeare Wrote for Money, Housekeeping vs. the Dirt,* and *The Polysyllabic Spree,* and editor of the short story collection *Speaking with the Angel*. A recipient of the American Academy of Arts and Letters' E. M. Forster Award, and the Orange Word International Writers' London Award, 2003, Hornby lives in North London.

Also by Nick Hornby

FICTION
HIGH FIDELITY
ABOUT A BOY
HOW TO BE GOOD
A LONG WAY DOWN
SLAM
JULIET, NAKED

NONFICTION
FEVER PITCH
SONGBOOK
THE POLYSYLLABIC SPREE
HOUSEKEEPING VS. THE DIRT
SHAKESPEARE WROTE FOR MONEY

ANTHOLOGY
SPEAKING WITH THE ANGEL

AN EDUCATION:
The Screenplay

Nick Hornby

RIVERHEAD BOOKS
New York

RIVERHEAD BOOKS
Published by the Penguin Group
Penguin Group (USA) Inc.
375 Hudson Street, New York, New York 10014, USA
Penguin Group (Canada), 90 Eglinton Avenue East, Suite 700, Toronto, Ontario M4P 2Y3, Canada
(a division of Pearson Penguin Canada Inc.)
Penguin Books Ltd., 80 Strand, London WC2R 0RL, England
Penguin Group Ireland, 25 St. Stephen's Green, Dublin 2, Ireland
(a division of Penguin Books Ltd.)
Penguin Group (Australia), 250 Camberwell Road, Camberwell, Victoria 3124, Australia
(a division of Pearson Australia Group Pty. Ltd.)
Penguin Books India Pvt. Ltd., 11 Community Centre, Panchsheel Park,
New Delhi—110 017, India
Penguin Group (NZ), 67 Apollo Drive, Rosedale, North Shore 0632, New Zealand
(a division of Pearson New Zealand Ltd.)
Penguin Books (South Africa) (Pty.) Ltd., 24 Sturdee Avenue, Rosebank, Johannesburg 2196,
South Africa

Penguin Books Ltd., Registered Offices: 80 Strand, London WC2R 0RL, England

The publisher does not have any control over and does not assume any responsibility for author or third-party websites or their content.

AN EDUCATION: THE SCREENPLAY

First Riverhead trade paperback edition: October 2009
Riverhead trade paperback ISBN: 978-1-59448-453-7

PRINTED IN THE UNITED STATES OF AMERICA

10 9 8 7 6 5 4 3 2 1

Contents

AN EDUCATION

INTRODUCTION

The First Draft

I knew the moment I'd finished Lynn Barber's wonderful autobiographical essay in *Granta*, about her affair with a shady older man at the beginning of the 1960s, that it had all the ingredients for a film. There were memorable characters, a vivid sense of time and place – an England right on the cusp of profound change – an unusual mix of high comedy and deep sadness, and interesting, fresh things to say about class, ambition and the relationship between children and parents. My wife, Amanda, is an independent film producer, so I made her read it, too, and she and her colleague Finola Dwyer went off to option it. It was only when they began to talk about possible writers for the project that I began to want to do it myself – a desire which took me by surprise, and which wasn't entirely welcome. Like just about every novelist I know, I have a complicated, usually unsatisfactory relationship with film writing: ever since my first book, *Fever Pitch*, was published, I have had some kind of script on the go. I adapted *Fever Pitch* for the screen myself, and the film was eventually made. But since then there have been at least three other projects – a couple of originals, and an adaptation of somebody else's work – which ended in failure, or at least in no end product, which is the same thing.

The chief problem with scriptwriting is that, most of the time, it seems utterly pointless, especially when compared with the relatively straightforward business of book publishing: the odds against a film, any film, ever being made are simply too great. Once you have established yourself as a novelist, then people seem quite amenable to the idea of publishing your books: your editor will make suggestions as to how they can be improved, of course, but the general idea is that, sooner or later, they will be in a bookshop, available for purchase. Film, however, doesn't work that way, not least because even the lower-budget films often cost millions of pounds to make, and as a consequence there is no screenwriter alive, however established in the profession, who writes in the secure knowledge that his work will be filmed. Plenty of people make a decent living from writing screenplays, but that's not quite the same thing: as a rule of thumb, I'd estimate that there is a 10 per cent chance of any movie actually being put into production, especially if one is working outside the studio system, as every writer in Britain does and must. I know, through my relationship with Amanda and Finola and other friends who work in the business, that London is awash with optioned books, unmade scripts, treatments awaiting development money that will never arrive.

So why bother? Why spend three, four, five years rewriting and rewriting a script that is unlikely ever to become a film? For me, the first reason to walk back into this world of pain, rejection and disappointment was the desire to collaborate: I spend much of my working day on my own, and I'm not naturally unsociable. Signing up for *An Education* initially gave me the chance to sit in a room with Amanda and Finola and Lynn and talk about the project as if it might actually happen one day, and later on I had similar conversations with directors and actors and the people from BBC Films. A novelist's life is devoid of meetings, and yet people with proper jobs get to go to them all the time. I suspect that part of the appeal of film for me is not only the opportunity for collaboration it provides, but the illusion it gives of real work, with colleagues and appointments and coffee cups with saucers and biscuits that I haven't bought myself. And there's one more big attraction: if it does come off, then it's proper fun, lively and glamorous and exciting in a way that poor old books can never be, however hard they try. Even before this film's release, we have taken it to the Sundance Festival in Utah, and Berlin. And I have befriended several of the cast, who, by definition, are better-looking than the rest of us . . . What has literature got, by comparison?

I wrote the first draft of *An Education* on spec, sometime in 2004, and while doing so, I began to see some of the problems that would have to be solved if the original essay were ever to make it to the screen. There were no problems with the essay itself, of course, which did everything a piece of memoir should do; but by its very nature, memoir presents a challenge, consisting as it does of an adult mustering all the wisdom he or she can manage to look back at an earlier time in life. Almost all of us become wiser as we get older, so we can see pattern and meaning in an episode of autobiography – pattern and meaning that we would not have been able to see at the time. Memoirists know it all, but the people they are writing about know next to nothing.

We become other things, too, as well as wise: more articulate, more cynical, less naïve, more or less forgiving, depending on how things have turned out for us. The Lynn Barber who wrote the memoir – a celebrated journalist, known for her perspicacious, funny, occasionally devastating profiles of celebrities – shouldn't be audible in the voice of the central character in our film, not least because, as Lynn says in her essay, it was the very experiences that she was describing that formed the woman we know. In other words, there was no 'Lynn Barber' until she had received the eponymous education. Oh, this sounds obvious to the point of banality: a sixteen-year-old girl should sound different from her sixty-year-old self. What is less obvious, perhaps, is the way the sixty-year-old self seeps into every brush-stroke of the self-portrait in a memoir. Sometimes even the dialogue that Lynn provided for her younger version – perfectly plausible on the page – sounded too hard-bitten, when I thought about a living, breathing young actress saying the words. I had been here before, in a way, with the adaptation of *Fever Pitch*. In a memoir, one tries to be as smart as one can about one's younger self – that's sort of what the genre is, and that's what Lynn had done. In a screenplay, however, one has to deny the subject that insight, otherwise there's no drama, just a character understanding herself and avoiding mistakes.

The other major problem was the ending. Lynn Barber nearly threw her life away, nearly missed out on the chance to go to university, nearly didn't sit her exams. And though lots of movie endings derive their power from close shaves, they tend to be a little more enthralling: the bullet just misses the hero, the meteor just misses our planet. It was going to be hard to make people care about whether a young girl got a place at Oxford, no matter how clever she was. Lynn became Jenny after the first draft or two; there were practical reasons for the change, but it helped me to think about the character that I was in the process of creating, rather than the character who existed already, the person who had written the piece of memoir: I could attempt to raise the stakes for Jenny, whereas I would have felt more obliged to stick to the facts if she had remained Lynn.

Some stories mean something, some don't. It was clear to me that this one did, but I wasn't sure what, and the things it meant to me weren't and couldn't be the same as the things it meant to Lynn: she had found, in this chapter of her life, all sorts of interesting clues to her future, for example, but I couldn't worry about my character's future. I had to worry about her present, and how that present might feel compelling to an audience. It would take me several more drafts before I got even halfway there.

BBC Films

The first time I had a formal conversation with outsiders in the film industry about *An Education*, it didn't go well. Somebody who was in a position to fund the film – because Amanda and Finola, as independent producers, do not and cannot do that – had expressed an interest, read my first draft, invited us in to a meeting. His colleague, however, clearly wasn't convinced that there was any potential in the film at all, and that was that. This reflected a pattern repeated many times over the next few years: there was interest in the script, followed by doubts about whether any investment could ever be recouped. Sometimes it felt as though I was in the middle of writing a little literary novel, and going around town asking for a £4 million advance for it. Our belief in the project, our conviction that it could one day become a beautiful thing, was sweet, and the producers' passion got us through a few doors, but it didn't mean that we weren't going to cost people money. Another problem with the film's commercial appeal was beginning to become apparent, too: the lead actress would have to be an unknown – no part for Kate or Cate or Angelina here – and no conventional male lead would want to play the part of the predatory, amoral, possibly lonely David, the older man who seduces the young girl. (Peter Sarsgaard, who responded and committed to the script at an early stage, is a proper actor: he didn't seem to worry much about whether his character would damage his chances of getting the lead in a romantic comedy.)

The good people at BBC Films, however, saw something in the script – either that, or the desperation in our eyes – and funded the development of *An Education*, which meant paying me to write another draft, and giving Amanda and Finola some seed money. The meeting we had with David Thompson and Tracey Scoffield went the way no conversations of this kind go, in my experience: as we talked, their professional scepticism was replaced by enthusiasm and understanding. This is supposed to be the point of meetings, from the supplicants' point of view, anyway; but in my experience (and probably in yours, too, whatever your profession), nobody who was previously doubtful is ever really open to persuasion or suggestion. The fact that the thirty minutes or so spent talking to David and Tracey wasn't a waste of time is more remarkable than it should be.

I didn't need money to write another draft of the script, of course; I am well paid in my other profession, and there's very little to be earned in British film, especially at this early stage. But money has a symbolic value, too. We all needed some indication that others in the industry felt as enthusiastic about *An Education* as we did, otherwise we could be pretty sure that any future energy poured into the project would run right through it and down the drain. BBC Films gave us a sense of purpose. They were not in a position to fund the film, but they could help us get the project into shape so that others might want to.

The Banana

In the original piece, and in the film itself, our heri-one's seducer produces a banana on the night he wants to take her virginity, apparently because he thinks it will result in ease of access. It was a strange and revealing detail that I wanted to keep, because it indicated something of David's gaucheness.

At a BBC script meeting, David Thompson, then head of BBC Films, started to muse aloud about this particular scene.

'The banana,' he said hesitantly. 'Could it . . . Would it work?'

He directed the question at Amanda and Finola. They shifted uncomfortably in their seats. There was a silence.

Jamie Laurenson, one of the executive producers, cleared his throat.

'I don't think . . . I don't think it would be a peeled banana,' he said.

'Ah!' said David. 'Unpeeled! I see.'

We moved on, gratefully.

Directors

It helps to attach a director to the project, too, for exactly the same reasons. Beeban Kidron read what-ever was the most recent draft, liked it, met to talk about it, and then worked with me on the script for the best part of a year. (These years slip by, so it's a relief to remember that other things were happening while *An Education* wasn't being made. I wrote my young adult novel *Slam*, and my third son was born; Finola was off making the HBO drama *Tsunami*. We have something to show for that time.) I loved working with Beeban, who lives round the corner from my office and could therefore meet within five minutes of receiving an email, if she was around; it was through talking to her, thinking about what she needed from the script as a film-maker, that I made several important improvements to the script. Certainly Jenny's complicity in many of David's deceptions, her willingness to manipulate her parents, came out of my work with Beeban; we took as our cue Lynn Barber's admission, in the original piece, that when she witnessed 'David' stealing the map, she didn't do anything about it. The decision we made during that time made the script more morally complicated, and the film is the richer for it.

Beeban and I had a cloud hanging over us, however. She was attached to another movie which, like ours, had spent a long time in development. Eventually it became apparent that she couldn't do both, that they were going to clash, and reluctantly (I think and hope) she decided to go with the project which had predated ours. We were back to square one.

We talked to several more directors after Beeban's departure. Most wanted to develop the script further, which was fair enough; the trouble is that no two directors could agree on the route we should be taking. One young director even wondered whether the whole 1962 thing was a red herring – had we thought of setting it in the present day? No, we hadn't. I was particularly keen to work with a woman director – yes, I had female producers to keep a watch on Jenny as she developed in the script, but the value of a woman director who could work with our young actress on set would, I felt, be incalculable – and when Lone Scherfig, the Danish director of *Italian for Beginners*, expressed an interest in making the film, we all wanted to listen to what she had to say. Lone turned out to be smart about the script, endlessly enthusiastic, and with an outsider's eye for detail; after she'd taken the job, she set about immersing herself in the look of 1962 England, its clothes and its cars and its cakes. We were lucky to find her.

The Cast

So then we were four: Amanda, Finola, Lone and I. And, for some time, we'd been talking to casting director Lucy Bevan. I'm quite often asked how much input I have in the various processes of film-making – 'Do you have a say in the casting, for example?' And though I'd like to claim credit for just about everything, the truth is that I simply don't know enough about actors (or directors, or editors, or designers, or composers) to contribute to these decisions in any meaningful way. How many young actresses did I know capable of playing the part of Jenny, for example? None at all. What about male actors for the part of David? Well, there was Colin Firth, of course, who I knew from *Fever Pitch*. And John Cusack (*High Fidelity*), and Hugh Grant and Nicholas Hoult from *About a Boy*, and the guy with the haircut from *No Country for Old Men*; which I'd just seen, probably, right before I was asked for my opinion . . . OK, not one of these was right, but they were all I could think of. Lucy Bevan's job is to read a script and come up with scores of imaginative suggestions for each part, and she's brilliant at it. On the whole, it's best that the casting director, rather than the writer, has a say in casting.

Every now and again I'd say, 'Oh God, you can't ask *him*.' Not because the actor in question was bad, or wrong for the part, but because it seemed to me insulting and embarrassing to offer it to him. Lucy, Amanda and Finola were ambitious for *An Education* in ways that I could never have been, which is why we ended up with Alfred Molina, Dominic Cooper and Rosamund Pike, rather than, say, me, my friend Harry and my next-door neighbour.

We were helped immeasurably by Emma Thompson agreeing to play the headmistress at an early stage: she gives any project an aura of authority and potential excellence. It was Lucy who knew about Carey Mulligan, of course – she's been in *Bleak House* and *Pride and Prejudice*, and those who had worked with her all talked of her phenomenal talent. But when I was told that they were thinking of casting a twenty-two-year-old as sixteen-year-old Jenny, I was a little disappointed (my exact words, Amanda tells me gleefully, were 'Well, that's ruined it all'); it would, I thought, be a different kind of film, with an older and as a consequence more knowing girl in the lead role. But when I saw the first shots of Carey in her school uniform, I worried that she looked too young, that we were involved in a dubious remake of *Lolita*. When Carey's mother visited the set, she told us that Carey had always cursed her youthful looks, but here they worked for her: I cannot imagine any other actress who could have been so convincing as a schoolgirl and yet so dazzling after her transformation. And, of course, she can act. This was a huge part for any young actress – Jenny is in every single scene – but I don't think one ever tires of watching her. There's so much detail, so much intelligence in the performance that it's impossible to get bored.

My only contribution was a small panic when I'd watched her audition on DVD – she was so clearly, uncannily right that I was concerned when I heard she hadn't yet been offered the role. And yet this small panic, expressed after producers and director and casting agent had seen the audition, and long after she'd been cast in other high-profile productions, is easily enough for me to claim that I discovered her; so I will, for years to come.

Orlando Bloom

'Oh God, you can't ask him,' I said. Well, they'd already asked him, and he'd already said he wanted to play the part of Danny. Arrangements were made for the care of his dog.

A couple of weeks before shooting, I was asked to talk to him about a couple of lines in the script. He called me at my office and told me that, much as he admired the writing, he wouldn't be able to play the part. He hoped we'd be able to work together on something else. Confused, I called my wife and told her that, as far as I could tell, Orlando Bloom had just told me he wouldn't, after all, be playing the part of Danny. Amanda spoke to his agent.

'No,' she said. 'There has been a misunderstanding.' (It was clear, I felt, from the tone of her voice, who had misunderstood whom.) 'He just wanted to talk to you about the script.'

I replayed the conversation in my head. We already had a wonderful cast lined up, but Orlando Bloom's fan club would, it was felt, help the box office of a small British film no end. How had I managed to drive him away, in under three minutes? What had I said?

'He's going to call you at home later,' she said. Don't mess it up, she didn't say. But that's what I heard anyway.

He called that night, and we had exactly the same conversation. I strode around our kitchen, listening to Orlando Bloom talk about his regret and sadness, while I made throat-chopping gestures at my wife. As I wasn't doing any of the talking, she could see and hear that I wasn't doing any of the damage, either. I have no idea what any of it was about – why he'd turned us down, why he'd said yes in the first place, whether he'd ever intended to do it, whether it really was Orlando Bloom I'd been speaking to.

Incredibly, the brilliant Dominic Cooper stepped in almost immediately.

The Read-Through

In the strange world of independent cinema, everyone – director, writer, cast, producers – proceeds on the basis that the film will be made, even though there is still no money with which to make it. If it's not make-believe (after all, we were all being paid to pretend, which children aren't), then it's a particularly committed form of method acting: we were inhabiting the bodies of independent film-makers, thinking their thoughts at all times in the hope of convincing someone that this was who we were. And eventually somebody believed us. The American financiers Endgame Entertainment liked the script and the cast and the director; this, together with the not insubstantial contribution of the BBC, was enough to enable the film to happen. So suddenly we were all sitting around a table, reading the script out loud to see how it sounded. (I say 'we' because I read, too – Alfred Molina couldn't make it, so I played the part of Jenny's father, Jack. This I did by shouting a lot.) I have been to a few read-throughs, and if they go well, as this one did, they are completely thrilling, not least because this is the only time that the script is read from beginning to end in its entirety, so it's the only chance the writer ever gets to listen to his words in the right order, in real time. The film isn't shot that way, and scenes get chopped, or never shot in the first place . . . For the writer, the read-through is the purest, most fully realised version of the script, before the actual film-making part of film-making gets in the way.

At one point in the afternoon, Matthew Beard, the brilliant young actor who plays Jenny's first boyfriend Graham, got a laugh from the word 'hello'; there was no such laugh in the script, and you suddenly see the point of a cast – while at the same time, of course, slightly resenting their talent.

The Shoot

I wasn't there much, so don't ask me. I had just started a book (*Juliet, Naked*, available now in all good bookshops), and wanted to make it longer; and in any case, being married to the producer of *An Education* played havoc with childcare arrangements. Some directors like to have the writer on set, but Lone didn't seem to need me much, not least because she was so gratifyingly determined to be faithful to the script as it was written. And in any case, any questions she might have had could always be asked via Amanda, who could pass them on, quite often late at night or over breakfast. Lone was always perfectly warm and friendly if I did show up, and actors are always interesting people to waste time with. But that's what filming is, time-wasting (even, most of the time, for a lot of the people directly involved); past experience has taught me that there is really no

15

other way to characterise it. Our budget was tight, so everyone had to move fast, but this still meant that several hours a day, literally, were spent moving lights around, or re-arranging furniture. In the words of Homer Simpson: 'I've seen plays that are more interesting. Seriously. *Plays*.' All a writer can really do is marvel that an activity so solitary, so imprecise and so apparently whimsical, can result, however many years later, in the teeming humanity of a film set.

The Ending

I was struck, in Lynn's original piece, by 'David' coming to find her in Oxford; it seemed like an appropriate ending for the film. And yet any event that happens after the main timeline of the script's narrative was always going to seem more like a coda than a climax – I can see that now, but it didn't seem so obvious during the writing nor the shooting of *An Education*. We shot the scene, and included it in all the early edits, but it never really worked: it didn't give the actors enough to do, apart from restate their positions with as much vehemence and/or self-delusion as they could muster. The actors, meanwhile, had effectively found their own ending. The bravura performances of Carey and Alfred Molina during the emotional climax of the film, in which Jack talks to Jenny through her bedroom door, and reveals that he and Jenny's mother had learned that the trip to Oxford had been a con trick, were enough, we felt; that, plus Jenny's smile to herself when she receives the letter from Oxford (a moment that wasn't scripted – it was something cooked up on the phone during the shoot). It all works, I think. But if you needed any further proof that film is a collaborative medium, here it is. That ending was created by Lone, Carey, Alfred and Barney Pilling, the editor. And me, I suppose, although not in the way I had intended to create it.

The Music

1962 was, I think, the last time that British youth looked across the Channel for inspiration, rather than across the Atlantic. The Beatles and the Stones existed, but hadn't released any records when Jenny met Peter; and yes, we could have used music by Little Richard or Elvis, but pop had no kind of cachet among the young, clever middle classes, not yet. 'I want to be French,' Jenny says – because she loves French music, French films, French food. London was on the verge of swinging, but only a select few could have felt the first sensation of movement; London right at the beginning of the sixties still bore more than a passing resemblance to its wartime self. It is strange to think, for example, that Jenny would have experienced the privations of food rationing for the first half of her life. This was one reason why the UK needed interpreters of American music like Lennon and McCartney, people to transform it so that it made sense: American rock'n'roll, with its cars and girls imagery, was a product of American post-war affluence, but Britain had been ruined by the war. An English teenager waited in the rain for a bus. Jenny's daddy didn't have a T-Bird – nobody's daddy did.

We wanted to give a sense of the uniqueness and the difference of this time aurally; that meant no electric guitars, no blue suede shoes. Jazz, chanteuses and classical music would all help place Jenny precisely in her cultural context. This didn't, however, make the music any cheaper.

Well-known songs can command in excess of £10,000 each for publishing and recording nights, and these sorts of sums are almost never within reach of an independent production. We lost one song by Juliette Greco because of the publisher's high demand; and we were only able to licence our final choice of Greco recordings – at a rate we could afford – after Lone and I wrote to the singer herself for permission.

Mostly this was music I knew very little about – it's salutary to be reminded that what one thinks of as personal taste, an aesthetic that has taken years to achieve, is actually little more than the inevitable product of being born in a certain place at a certain time.

The Film

So, was it worth it? Yes, as far as I'm concerned, emphatically so. I am as proud of *An Education* as of anything I've ever written – prouder, if anything, if only because it's so much easier to take pride in other people's work. Whatever I think of the writing, I love the work of the actors, and Lone's direction, and

Andrew McAlpine's beautiful design, and John de Borman's camerawork, and if nothing else, I can take enormous pleasure in helping to create a structure in which this work was possible. 'You probably can't wait to start another one,' somebody said to me after the Sundance Festival, where *An Education* was received well and won a couple of awards. It should work like that, of course. But the simple fact of the film's existence, let alone any quality it might have, is miraculous, a freakish combination of the right material and the right people and an awful lot of tenacity, almost none of which was mine. And how many miracles does one have the right to expect, during the average working life?

SUNDANCE DIARY

Saturday, 17 January

The story so far: An Education, *a film with a script I adapted from a piece of Lynn Barber memoir which originally appeared in* Granta, *has been invited to the Sundance Film Festival.* An Education, *directed by Lone Scherfig, stars Peter Sarsgaard and Carey Mulligan, a brilliant young actress, and was produced by Finola Dwyer and my wife, Amanda Posey. Now read on . . .*

Amanda, Finola and I fly from LA to Salt Lake City. Utah is, I think, the twenty-third US state I have visited, and one I wasn't sure I'd ever get to: for some reason, they tend not to send me there on book tours. Park City, where most of Sundance happens, is up in the mountains some forty-five minutes' drive from Salt Lake City; there is thick snow everywhere, but the sun shines bright and warm every day of our visit. The snow thus becomes something of a mystery. In London it would have turned to an unappealing grey sludge before vanishing altogether. We dump our bags in the hotel, which also doubles as the Festival's HQ, and head straight off out to see a movie that we've been invited to by its screenwriters. We have two tickets between the three of us, and the screening is completely sold out, but when we get to the cinema my wife explains plaintively that Finola has dropped hers in the snow somewhere. I wince, and then remember that it's only through desperate lies like this that *An Education* got made at all. The flustered usherette waves us through, and we all find seats. The film, *500 Days of Summer*, is great, fresh and funny and true in a way that romantic comedies rarely are.

Afterwards, we catch a shuttle bus from the cinema to a party for the movie. The bus is packed, and everyone is talking about film; in the gangway next to us, a young cinematographer is chatting animatedly to a Canadian documentary maker. In five years' time the two of them will probably be onstage at the Oscar ceremony, remembering this first fortuitous meeting tearfully. We're English, though (Finola is from New Zealand, but similar national stereotypes apply), so we don't talk to anybody, apart from each other. That's why we won't be advancing our Hollywood careers this weekend.

At the party, we are all told several times that there is a tremendous buzz around our film. There are two sources for this: one was an enormously helpful and sincerely enthusiastic preview piece by the respected film critic Kenneth Turan in the *LA Times*, in which he described *An Education* as 'probably the jewel of the festival's dramatic films, and sure to be one of the best films of the year'; the other is that the film is premiering at the small Egyptian cinema, rather than the 1,400-seater where we saw *500 Days of Summer*. Nobody can get tickets, and this only increases our desirability. I can now see that booking us in the smaller cinema was a stroke of PR genius. We're the best film nobody can see.

We eat at a Thai restaurant around the corner from the party. We bump into my (English) film agent and two of her (English) colleagues; there are English film-makers at the table behind us. There are twelve English films from these islands on at the festival, a record.

Sunday, 18 January

I meet my friend Serge, of the rock band Marah, for a coffee. He lives in Salt Lake City with his wife, and they are expecting a baby now, this minute. I've got them both tickets for the screening, but they have no idea whether they'll be able to use them. Serge tells me that twenty years ago, Park City was a proper gold-rush ghost town; now it's a thriving, cute, middle-class ski-resort, full of smart gift shops and restaurants, like a snowy Henley-on-Thames. Those who have been before, like the actor Dominic Cooper (who, like Carey, has two films on at the festival – he is in ours and Brief Interviews with Hideous Men, an adaptation of the David Foster Wallace book), tell us that this year it's much quieter, and therefore much nicer – the state of the economy has reduced Sundance attendances by a third, some reckon. But the streets are crowded and the movies are all selling out, so it feels like any more people than this would be unnecessary. The puffy jackets and the ski-hats flatten everybody out, turn the film stars into normal people; you can be walking behind a perfectly ordinary-looking man striding out on his own, and then watch him stop to have his photo taken by someone walking towards you, someone who has the advantage of seeing his face. (Well, that happened once. It was Robin Williams.)

Our screening is at 3 p.m. We meet up with the director Lone Scherfig, and Carey, and people from Endgame, the US financiers, in the green room, and now I'm properly nervous. Of course, just as you have to share the credit if a film turns out OK, you can deflect the blame if it goes wrong: it was miscast, badly edited, the performances were poor, it was under-funded, and so on. And actually, if it goes right, it will be Lone who attracts most of the praise. But this is a family affair: my wife and I will both be depressed if it goes down like a lead zeppelin (and doesn't that spelling look *weird*?). And we were the ones who started this whole stupid, misbegotten project in the first place. I was the one who first read Lynn's original piece, and Amanda and Finola optioned it. We are entirely the authors of our own misfortune.

We take our seats, but there's a long delay while people mill around looking for empty places. The tickets at Sundance aren't numbered, and some people have passes that get them in to any screening they fancy, which inevitably means that attendances can exceed capacity. Lone is standing by the side of the stage, waiting to introduce the film, so her seat is empty; three times a stressed-out official tries to fill it.

I look for Serge, but can't find him. I imagine him in a hospital in Salt Lake, urging his wife to remember her breathing. I wish we were having a baby this afternoon.

I have seen the film twice before, once in its finished version, and both times it has been difficult for me to read how it's playing. The first two-thirds contain jokes, and on a good day people laugh at them; the last third is more serious, and intended to move an audience. In other words, the last half-hour is an agony of silence. (I often wonder whether I have always written would-be comic novels simply because it helps me ascertain whether people are awake at readings.) Three people leave in the second half of the film. Two of them come back (one of them, I realise, was Carey). I hate the third. I remember a story that a friend with a bad Sundance experience told me: he said that during a screening of one of his films a few years ago, all he could hear was the sound of slapping seats, as industry professionals decided that they'd seen enough to make their minds up. We fared better than that – you could definitely hear the soundtrack – but when the credits came up, I still wasn't at all sure how we'd done.

Lone, Carey, Dominic and I go onstage for the Q&A – the people who've stayed for it seem genuinely taken by the film, which is a relief. Afterwards, I go outside to smoke round the back of the cinema, and Lone, our Danish director, introduces me to a compatriot, a woman who is a juror on the awards panel.

'Hello,' I say. 'I hope you enjoyed it.'

I know she's a juror, but it wouldn't kill her to lie politely, I think. To tell a screenwriter that you enjoyed his film is not the same thing as telling him that you will shower him with prizes.

'I cannot tell you that,' she says firmly.

'Oh.'

I try to think of another pleasantry that will not compromise her obviously formidable integrity.

'Well . . . Thanks for coming.'

'I had no choice,' she says, but she still seems to expect a chat.

I shrug helplessly. 'I've got nothing left,' I tell her. She walks away.

I check my phone to see if Serge has left a message about Monica going into labour, and it turns out that they came to the screening but couldn't get anywhere near it. The tickets we had worked hard to get them were useless. There's another message from Scott, one the co-writers of 500 *Days of Summer*. His tickets were no good either. We only invited four friends, and none of them got inside the cinema.

One of the points – the chief point – of premiering the film at Sundance is to try and sell the film to an American distributor. *An Education* was made without any distribution already in place, which means that there was no guarantee that anyone would ever see it in a cinema, a fate that befalls a surprisingly large number of movies. To our delight, we had sold it for UK release shortly before the festival, but the US financiers need American distribution. It's not our problem, but of course we all want it, too: it's been made for people to watch, on a big screen. Everything I had read in the trade press about Sundance in the run-up to the Festival contained dire warnings about the economy's impact on sales; nobody was expecting much to happen. Our sales agents were confident that they'd get something, but they thought it would take time, that distributors would need to see all the movies before committing themselves to one or two. We were prepared not to hear anything for a week or two. But when we get to the strange and rather cheerless village hall that is our post-film party venue, we hear that an offer has already been made. We are jubilant. It turns out that it is a very bad offer – insulting, even, if you know enough to be insulted, which I don't. So I remain jubilant, like an idiot.

At the party I am introduced to David Carr, whose brilliant memoir *Night of the Gun* was one of my favourite books of last year: he wants to speak to me for his *New York Times* blog. It doesn't seem right. The book is so great that I feel I should be interviewing him.

He starts with an apology.

'I'm sorry,' he said. 'I had to leave your film halfway through. I was called out to interview Robert Redford.' The man who didn't come back was David Carr, author of *Night of the Gun*! And he had a good excuse anyway! I can now account for 100 per cent of the leavers: two weak bladders (or in Carey's case, completely understandable nerves) and a summons from a megastar.

When we get back to the hotel late that night, Amanda tells me that there is quite a lot going on: the insulting offer has been superseded by several less insulting offers. Distributors liked the film, and some of them want to buy it.

Monday, 19 January

Lone, Carey, Dominic and I have a day of publicity. It becomes apparent quite quickly that Carey's life has changed this weekend; her other film ended up getting mixed reviews, but her performance was praised to the skies, and everybody loves her in ours, too – which is just as well, seeing as she's in every single scene. Within twenty-four hours she's being described as the Sundance 'It' Girl in *Variety*, and 'the new Audrey Hepburn' in the *New York Post*. It's exciting to watch – like something out of an earlier, more glamorous age. As we walk through the Park City streets from appointment to appointment, several people want their photographs taken with her. She remains remarkably composed throughout the weekend. She's a very bright girl, and I am certain that she will be able to handle this year with grace and charm.

Lone and I are interviewed together by a young woman from a news agency. For some reason, the news agency has positioned itself for the duration of the festival on the second floor of a guitar shop, in what looks like a broom cupboard; underneath them, rock bands are playing short, loud sets. It's as if they have deliberately chosen the worst spot in Utah for recorded interviews. It takes us about half-an-hour to push through the music fans to the cupboard, and when we get inside it, it's obvious that the young woman hasn't emerged to see any films.

'Tell us about your characters,' is her opening shot.

'Lone's very calm,' I tell her. 'But I can be moody.'

She looks confused.

'We're not actors,' I confess.

Flustered, she consults her notes.

'It must be hard, working together when you're married. Was there any tension?'

'We're not married,' says Lone. Still. Where would we be without the press?

In the evening, Carey, Amanda, Finola and I go to see another film, and then attend yet another party. I think I have been to more parties here than in the whole of 2008. By now it's obvious that things have gone much better for us than we dared hope: the reviews we've seen have been unbelievable (one of the first, on the normally snarky 'LA gossip rag' Defamer.com, I wouldn't have dared write myself), the film is almost certainly going to sell for a decent amount, and to cap it all, here I am giving Uma Thurman a light. I don't have a lighter, so I hand her my cigarette. (I can only just reach – she's about a metre taller than me.)

'If you can live with the intimacy that implies,' she says.

And then I woke up.

I am always on the verge of giving up smoking, but my habit has resulted in my meeting both Uma (as I now think of her) and Kurt Vonnegut. Where's the incentive?

Amanda and Finola sign an agreement with Sony Picture Classics in the Virgin lounge at the San Francisco airport. When we get home we are told that *An Education* won the Audience Award and a prize for John de Borman's cinematography. Nothing from the Danish juror, though.

CAST AND CREW

Cast (in order of appearance)

Jenny CAREY MULLIGAN
Miss Stubbs OLIVIA WILLIAMS
Jack ALFRED MOLINA
Marjorie CARA SEYMOUR
Graham MATTHEW BEARD
David PETER SARSGAARD
Hattie AMANDA FAIRBANK-HYNES
Tina ELLIE KENDRICK
Danny DOMINIC COOPER
Helen ROSAMUND PIKE
Headmistress EMMA THOMPSON
Sarah SALLY HAWKINS
Nightclub Singer BETH ROWLEY

BBC FILMS PRESENTS

IN ASSOCIATION WITH ENDGAME ENTERTAINMENT

A WILDGAZE FILMS / FINOLA DWYER PRODUCTION

A FILM BY LONE SCHERFIG

Casting Director LUCY BEVAN
Line Producer CAROLINE LEVY
Music Supervisor KLE SAVIDGE

Makeup & Hair Designer LIZZIE YIANNI GEORGIOU
Costume Designer ODILE DICKS-MIREAUX
Music by PAUL ENGLISHBY
Editor BARNEY PILLING
Production Designer ANDREW MCALPINE
Director of Photography JOHN DE BORMAN BSC
Executive Producers JAMES D. STERN, DOUGLAS E.
HANSEN, WENDY JAPHET, DAVID M. THOMPSON,
JAMIE LAURENSON, NICK HORNBY
Based on a Memoir by LYNN BARBER
Screenplay by NICK HORNBY
Produced by FINOLA DWYER & AMANDA POSEY
Directed by LONE SCHERFIG

AN EDUCATION:
The Screenplay

1   INTERIOR: SCHOOL – DAY

Montage: A nice girls' school in a south-west London suburb. We see girls doing what girls did in a nice girls' school in 1961: walking with books on their heads, practising their handwriting, making cakes, playing lacrosse, dancing with each other.

2   INTERIOR: CLASSROOM – DAY

In one of the classrooms, MISS STUBBS, *an attractive, bright, animated schoolteacher, is talking to a small group of sixteen-year-old girls. Some of these girls seem to be daydreaming – looking out of the window, examining their fingernails. A couple, including a bespectacled girl* (ANN), *who looks five years younger than everyone else in the class, write down everything the teacher says. Only one,* JENNY, *beautiful and as animated as her teacher, seems to be listening in the spirit in which* MISS STUBBS *would like her to listen. She's smiling, eyes shining – she loves* MISS STUBBS *and these lessons.* MISS STUBBS *asks a question and looks at the girls for a response.*

      MISS STUBBS
      Anybody? . . .
JENNY *puts up her hand – the only person in class to do so.*
      Anybody else? . . .

No one else reacts.

> (mock-sighing)
> Yes. Jenny . . .

JENNY

Isn't it because Mr Rochester's blind?

3   INTERIOR: JENNY'S HOUSE – DAY

Title: TWICKENHAM, LONDON 1961
JENNY, *her mother and her father are finishing Sunday
lunch. Jenny's father,* JACK, *is in his forties;* MARJORIE,
her mother, is slightly younger than JACK, *but every bit as
middle-aged. The food is grey and brown, in keeping with
the colour scheme of the house. They aren't talking –
they're listening to Mantovani on the radio.* JENNY *gets
up from the lunch table.*

> JENNY
>
> I've got an English essay to do by tomorrow
> morning.

> JACK
>
> Right. So, the only sound I want to hear
> coming through the ceiling this afternoon
> is the sound of sweat dripping onto text-
> books.

> JENNY
> Cello?

JACK

No cello.

JENNY

I thought we agreed that cello was my interest or hobby.

JACK

Well, it already is your interest or hobby. So
when they ask you at the Oxford interview
'What is your interest or hobby?' you can
say, 'The cello' and you wouldn't be lying. But
you don't have to practise a hobby. A hobby
is a hobby.

JENNY

Can I stop going to the youth orchestra, then?

JACK

No, no, no. The youth orchestra's a good
thing. Shows you're a joiner-inner.

JENNY

Ah. Yes. But. I've already joined in. So now I
can stop.

JACK

No, no. Well, that just shows the opposite,
don't you see? That shows you're a rebel.
They don't want that at Oxford.

JENNY

No. They don't want people who think for
themselves.

JACK

(*missing the sarcasm, as is his wont*)
'Course they don't.

4   INTERIOR: SCHOOL HALL – DAY

JENNY *with cello sits in the string section. Everyone is
getting settled, tuning up, latecomers still arriving.
Along the row from* JENNY, *tuning his violin, is a
nice-looking boy of her age,* GRAHAM, *and she
waves at him. Two thirteen-year-old boys sitting
between them wave, too, parodically, and then blow
kisses, much to* GRAHAM'S *embarrassment and*
JENNY'S *fury.*

*The silly boys dissolve in fits of giggles: this is clearly
one of the funniest moments of their lives – until one of
them farts noisily and, it would appear from all the
frantic gesturing, pungently. The comic value of the fart
tops even the comic value of the wave, and they are
scarcely able to stay seated, such is their mirth.*

5   EXTERIOR: SCHOOL – DAY

JENNY *and* GRAHAM *are talking while he struggles to
take his bike out of a bicycle rack, slightly unbalanced by*

the violin strapped to his back. GRAHAM *is nervous, chronically unconfident and shy.*

GRAHAM

Should I wear, you know, Sunday best?

JENNY

You'd better, I'm afraid. Just to show my father you're *un jeune homme serieux,* not a teddy boy.

GRAHAM

Oh, God.

JENNY

(looking up at the sky)
I'm going to go. It's going to bucket down in a minute.

GRAHAM

Oh, OK, right . . .

JENNY

I'll see you at the weekend.

GRAHAM

Bye, then.

JENNY

Bye.

They move at the same time and bump awkwardly into each other.

JENNY/GRAHAM

Sorry.

The two silly boys from before are sitting on the school wall and start to blow more kisses.

SMALLER BOY 1

Goodbye, my love!

GRAHAM *blushes as he and* JENNY *head off in opposite directions.*

6   EXTERIOR: BUS STOP – DAY

The rain has begun. JENNY *attempts to cover herself. A mother pushing a pram and holding the hand of her little boy crosses the road in front of her, and a beautiful, sleek red sports car – a Bristol – stops to let them across.* DAVID, *possibly in his mid-thirties, dapper, and almost but not quite handsome, is driving the car.* DAVID, *distracted, impatient, spots* JENNY *at the bus stop.*
　　In front of the car a small Wellington boot drops off the foot of the boy, further slowing down their painfully slow progress across the road.
　　JENNY *is wet.* DAVID *makes eye contact.* JENNY *smiles ruefully and enchantingly. Once the mother and boy have crossed the road,* DAVID *pulls the car over by the bus stop and rolls the window of the Bristol down.*

40

DAVID

Hello.

JENNY *ignores him.*

Look. If you've any sense, you wouldn't take a lift from a strange man.

JENNY *smiles thinly.*

But I'm a music lover, and I'm worried about your cello. So what I propose is, you put it in the car and walk alongside me.

JENNY

How do I know you won't just drive off with the cello?

DAVID

Ah. Good point. How much does a new cello cost? Ten pounds? Fifteen? I don't know. Let's say fifteen.

He pulls out a wallet, takes out three five-pound notes, hands them to her.

JENNY *laughs and waves the money away.*

No? All right . . . Up to you.

DAVID *gets out of the car to help Jenny with the cello.*

I'm David, by the way.

JENNY

(*hesitates*)
Jenny.

DAVID

Very good.

He gets back in the car.

7 EXTERIOR: STREET, NEAR SCHOOL – DAY

*Moments later. The cello is in the backseat of the Bristol.
JENNY is trotting alongside the car, while DAVID leans
nonchalantly across the passenger seat to talk to her
while driving.*

DAVID

How did the concert go?

JENNY

It was a rehearsal. The concert's next Thursday.

DAVID

What are you playing?

JENNY

(*making a face*)
Elgar.

DAVID

Ah, Elgar. I think it's a shame he spent so much time in Worcester, don't you? Worcester's too near Birmingham. And you can

43

hear that in the music. There's a horrible
Brummy accent in there, if you listen hard
enough.

JENNY *looks at him and smiles. She hadn't expected him
to be able to make Elgar jokes.*

Anyway, Elgar and the Jews don't mix very
well.

JENNY
I'm not a Jew!

DAVID
(*laughing*)
No. I am. I wasn't . . . *accusing* you.

JENNY
Oh. (*She smiles awkwardly.*) Can I sit in the
car with my cello?

DAVID *stops the car.*

DAVID
Jump in.

8   INTERIOR: DAVID'S CAR – DAY

JENNY *shuts the door and sinks approvingly into the
leather seat.* DAVID *regards the dripping girl with
amusement.*

JENNY

I have never seen a car like this before. *C'est très chic.*

DAVID

It's a Bristol. Not many of 'em made.

JENNY *struggles for something to say.*

JENNY

Oh.

DAVID

Where to, madam?

JENNY *makes a face.*

JENNY

I only live round the corner. (*She pauses.*) Worse luck.

DAVID

I'll see what I can do.

DAVID *changes gear to slow the car down.*

9   EXTERIOR: DAVID'S CAR/STREET NEAR JENNY'S HOUSE – DAY

The Bristol is crawling along the road at walking pace.

INTERIOR/EXTERIOR: DAVID'S CAR, JENNY'S HOUSE – DAY

DAVID

I suppose cellists must go to a lot of concerts.

JENNY

We don't go to any concerts. We don't believe in them.

DAVID

Oh, they're real.

JENNY

So people say.

DAVID

Smoke?

DAVID *reaches across* JENNY *while driving slowly, opens the glove compartment and takes out a packet of cigarettes.*

JENNY

I'd better not.
(*indicating*)
I live just up there.

DAVID *pulls over near* JENNY'S *house.*

DAVID

Why don't we believe in them?

JENNY

He'd say there's no point to them.

DAVID *lights a cigarette.*

DAVID

Your father, this is?

JENNY

(*darkly*)
Oh, yes. They're just for fun. Apart from
school concerts, of course, which are no fun
at all, so we go to those. The proper ones
don't help you *get on.*

DAVID

Which, of course, is what is so wonderful
about them. Anyway, you'll go one day.

JENNY

(*heartfelt*)
I know, I will. If I get to university, I'm going
to read what I want and listen to what I want.
And I'm going to look at paintings and watch
French films and talk to people who know
lots about lots.

DAVID

Good for you.

JENNY

(*laughing*)
Yes.

DAVID

Which university?

JENNY

Oxford. If I'm lucky. Did you go anywhere?

DAVID

I studied at what I believe they call the University of Life. And I didn't get a very good degree there.

JENNY *smiles.*

JENNY

Well . . . Thank you for driving me home.

She gets out of the car and takes the cello. DAVID *stares after her for a moment, then drives off. We start to hear . . .*

II   INTERIOR: JENNY'S BEDROOM – DAY

. . . Juliette Greco 'Sous le Ciel de Paris'. The sound of the French music plays as we pan across JENNY'S *bedroom to find her singing along, next to her Dansette record player.*

Suddenly there's a thumping noise – someone underneath her is banging on the ceiling impatiently.

JACK (*out of sight*)

I don't want to hear French singing. French
singing wasn't on the syllabus, last time I
looked.

JENNY *sighs and reaches for the volume control. She
turns the music down so low that she has to lie down and
put her head right next to the Dansette to hear it.*

Close on JENNY *as she silently mouths the words along
with the almost inaudible track.*

12   INTERIOR: JENNY'S HOUSE –
AFTERNOON

JENNY, *her parents and* GRAHAM *are eating afternoon
tea – neat fish-paste sandwiches, Battenberg cake, best
china.*

MARJORIE

Battenberg?

GRAHAM

Thank you. (*As* MARJORIE *serves, the cake
breaks up.*) I actually like the crust.

JACK

So where are you applying, Graham?

JENNY *looks embarrassed. She knows what's coming.*

GRAHAM

I'm not sure yet.

JACK

When will you be sure? You can't let the grass
grow under your feet, young man.

GRAHAM

I might take a year off.

JENNY *winces.* JACK *looks at him as if he's just said he'll
take all his clothes off.*

JACK

What for?

GRAHAM

(*mumbling*)
I don't know. Maybe do some travelling.

JACK

Travelling? What are you, a teddy boy?
Close-up of JENNY— *she knows what's coming, and can't
bear it. Beat.*

JACK

(*nodding at* JENNY)
You know she's going to Oxford, don't you?
If we can get her Latin up to scratch.

JENNY *sighs.*

So she's studying English at Oxford while
you'll be the wandering Jew . . .

JENNY *looks at him curiously.* GRAHAM *steels himself to
speak.*

50

GRAHAM

Mr Mellor . . . I'm not a teddy boy. I'm an *homme serieux. Jeune.* No. Yeah. I'm a *homme jeune serieux homme.*

JENNY *winces again. Her father stares at* GRAHAM. GRAHAM *blushes.*

13 EXTERIOR: JENNY'S HOUSE – EVENING

It's the day of the youth orchestra concert. JENNY, *her mother and her father are on their way out of the door.* JENNY *is in her school uniform, with her hair scrubbed back in a severe ponytail and is carrying her cello.* JENNY *opens the front door.*

MARJORIE

Ooh!

MARJORIE *and* JENNY *have seen something on the doorstep, and* JENNY *stoops to pick it up – a large basket of flowers.*

JENNY

They're for me!

MARJORIE

(*curious*)

Who are they from?

JENNY *opens the card that's attached to the handle.*

JENNY

Gosh. Him.

JACK *leans over* JENNY *and stares at the flowers in disbelief. The bunch of flowers has created in* JACK *the kind of panic and fear more typically associated with a biochemical attack.*

JACK

What's this?

MARJORIE

(*drily, knowing the trouble this will cause*)
Jack, I'm afraid Jenny has been sent some flowers from a chap.

JACK

A chap? What kind of chap?

JENNY

(*patiently*)
He's wishing me luck for tonight.

JACK

Is that all he's wishing you? Where does he get the money from?

JENNY

He earns it, I expect.

JACK

Earns it? Why isn't he at school?

JENNY

Can we just go? Otherwise the good-luck
flowers will actually be responsible for me
actually missing the concert. Which would be
ironic, *n'est ce pas?*

JACK

I don't like it.

MARJORIE

Objection noted. Jenny?

JENNY

Noted.

Gesturing at the flowers.

JACK

There's got to be ten bob's worth of luck
here. That's a bit much for a schoolgirl, isn't
it? You can't leave it out. Even *I'd* burgle a
house that had flowers outside. They'll think
we're made of money.

MARJORIE *puts them inside the house, shuts the door.*

Thank you, Marjorie.

14   INTERIOR: COFFEE BAR – DAY

JENNY *and two school friends,* HATTIE *and* TINA, *are
sitting at a table in a typical late-'50s coffee bar, sipping*

cappuccinos. JENNY *is easily the most attractive of the three — and also, we will see, possibly the cleverest.* HATTIE *is slower than the other two and a lot frumpier;* TINA *is pretty and sharp rather than clever. She is also the least middle-class of the three — she's clearly a scholarship girl. They are all dressed in an unflattering and unambiguous school uniform — no attempts to disguise it with more fashionable accessories.*

JENNY *is holding a copy of Camus'* The Outsider *and smoking pretentiously, and seems to be practising some kind of pout.* TINA *starts to slurp the froth from her cappuccino with a spoon, inelegantly and noisily.* JENNY *tuts her disapproval.* TINA *sighs and puts her spoon down.*

JENNY

Camus doesn't want you to like him. Feeling is bourgeois. Being *engagé* is bourgeois. He kills someone and he doesn't feel anything. His mother dies and he doesn't feel anything.

TINA

I wouldn't feel anything if my mother died. Does that make me an existentialist?

JENNY

No. That makes you a cow.

HATTIE

Une vache.

Laughter.

JENNY, HATTIE *and* TINA *emerge from the café, talking.*

> JENNY
>
> After I've been to university I'm going to *be* French. I'm going to Paris and I'm going to smoke and listen to Jacques Brel. And I won't speak. Ever. *C'est plus chic, comme ça* . . .

She breaks off. Parked outside a tobacconist's booth on the other side of the road is the red Bristol. She looks towards the booth, and DAVID *emerges with a copy of the* Times *and a packet of cigars.*

> Oh, crikey!
> (*to Hattie and Tina*)
> Wait here.

JENNY *crosses the road to talk to him while the others watch.*

> DAVID
>
> Hello.

> JENNY
>
> Hello. Thank you.

> DAVID
>
> How did it go?

> JENNY
>
> Oh, fine. I think. I mean, I didn't mess my bit up. And no one got thrown out of the orchestra afterwards.

DAVID

Always the mark of a cultural triumph. Listen. I'm glad I ran into you. What are you doing on Friday?

JENNY

Going to school.

DAVID

I meant the evening.

JENNY

(*embarrassed*)
Oh. Yes. Of course. Nothing.

DAVID

Because I'm going to listen to some Ravel in St John's, Smith Square. My friends Danny and Helen will be going, too, so it wouldn't be . . . I'll tell you what. I'll come and pick you up, and if your mother and father disapprove, then you can have the tickets and go with one of them. How does that sound?

JENNY *doesn't know what to say. She looks at*
DAVID, *and his eagerness to please seems to convince her.*

JENNY

Thank you. And I'd like to go with you.

DAVID

Seven? And we'll probably go for a spot of supper afterwards.

JENNY

(*flat disbelief*)
Supper.

DAVID

If you want to.

JENNY

The trouble is, we'll probably have eaten.

DAVID

Well, if you'd like supper, then, perhaps on Friday you could . . . not eat?

JENNY

(*embarrassed again*)
Oh. Yes. Of course.

JENNY *smiles and rejoins her friends on the other side of the road.* TINA *and* HATTIE *are standing there almost with their mouths open, amazed. She doesn't say anything and starts to walk on.* TINA *and* HATTIE *run to catch up.*

TINA

(*shrieking*)
A spot of supper?

JENNY

You've heard of supper?

HATTIE

We've *heard* of it. But we've never eaten it.

They walk off, giggling.

You're going to have to tell us everything.
Otherwise it's not fair . . .

16 INTERIOR: JENNY'S HOUSE –
EVENING

JENNY *is dressed up for her evening out. She looks good,
but also stiff, uncomfortable – she's not herself in her
dress, which looks too old for her. Her father is sitting at
the dining table, shouting.*

JACK

I won't allow it!

JENNY

(*coolly*)
Fine. He's more than happy for you to take
me.

JACK

(*uncertainly*)
Fine. I will.

JENNY

Good.

MARJORIE *comes into the room.*

JACK

Where is it?

JENNY

St John's, Smith Square.

JACK

Where's that?

JENNY

I don't know. I'm sure we could find out.

MARJORIE

It's in Westminster. Just around the corner
from the Abbey.

JACK *looks at her as if she'd just given directions to the
nearest opium den.*

JACK

How d'you know that?

MARJORIE

I had a life before we were married, you know.

JENNY

He soon put a stop to that.

JACK

Well, there we are.

JENNY

Where are we?

JACK

Near Westminster Abbey. I'm not going all
the way over there.

JENNY

The trouble is, that's where St John's, Smith
Square is.

JACK

There must be something on locally. Where's
the paper?

MARJORIE

Jack, she wants to see someone who can play.
She doesn't want to see Sheila Kirkland
scratching away. I'll take her.

JACK

And how do you suppose to get there? RAF
helicopter?

The doorbell rings.

JENNY

That's him.

JACK

Oh, bloody hell.

MARJORIE

Jack!

JENNY *starts towards the door, and then turns.*

JENNY

Oh, and by the way . . . David's a Jew.
A wandering Jew. So watch yourself.

She goes to the door.

JACK

(*panic-stricken and shouting*)
What does she mean by that? I've never said
anything like that! It's just an expression. I've
got nothing against the Jews . . .

JENNY *comes back in with* DAVID, *who seems intimidatingly exotic. He has obviously heard* JACK´S *last line.*

DAVID

(*pleasantly*)
I'm glad to hear it. Hello. David.

He offers his hand.

JACK

I didn't mean I've got nothing against *you* . . .
Actually, I did mean that, but . . .

DAVID'S *hand is still extended – in his confusion and
embarrassment,* JACK *hasn't yet taken it. He does so now
and shakes it for way too long.*

I'm sorry. What I'm saying is that you're not the sort of, of person I'd be against, if I were the sort of person who was against . . . people . . . Oh, dear. I'm Jack, and this is Marjorie.

DAVID

(*deadpan*)
You didn't tell me you had a sister, Jenny.
General confusion, until David chuckles naughtily.
MARJORIE *giggles, and then offers her hand.*
You're a lucky man, Jack.

JACK
I suppose I am, yes.
They all sit down.

DAVID
(*looking around approvingly*)
This is lovely.
MARJORIE *smiles.*

MARJORIE
Thank you.

JACK
I'm sorry, David. Would you like a drink?

DAVID
I'd love one, Jack, but we're running a little late. If Jenny's ready, perhaps we'll shoot off.

JENNY *looks at her father and takes a calculated gamble.*

> JENNY
>
> Actually, David, Dad has something he has to tell you.

> JACK
>
> No, no, nothing . . . It was more of a question, really. A point of reference. What's the best way to get to St John's, Smith Square from here?

> DAVID
>
> Oh, it's a pretty straight run, really. Up to Hammersmith, take the A4 through Kensington and you're there.

> JACK
>
> Simple as that.

> DAVID
>
> Simple as that.

JACK *smiles broadly.*

> MARJORIE
>
> (*playfully*)
> Shall I book us some tickets?

> JACK
>
> (*still smiling*)
> No.

Beat.

> Have her back by ten, David.

> DAVID

> Well, I was hoping she might come with me afterwards for a spot of supper with my aunt Helen.

JENNY *studies him carefully. Suddenly his friends* DANNY *and* HELEN *have become 'Aunt Helen'.*

> JACK

> Oh, well, er . . . No, she's usually in bed by then.

JENNY *winces.*

> DAVID

> What if I promise to have her back by eleven thirty?

> JACK

> Well, it's Friday night. And you *are* going all the way to the West End . . .

> DAVID

> Thanks, Jack. I appreciate it.

They exchange warm handshakes. He turns to MARJO-RIE, *who extends her hand.* DAVID *takes it, but kisses it suavely, leaving her a little flustered.*

JENNY

Bye.

JENNY *and* DAVID *leave.*

17   EXTERIOR: ST JOHN'S, SMITH SQUARE – EVENING

JENNY *and* DAVID *run in the rain toward the beautiful hall.* JENNY *suddenly looks young in the dress that looks too old for her – other adults are milling around outside, and the women don't look like girls dressed up.* DAVID *makes for an incredibly glamorous and attractive couple in their late twenties who are waiting outside –* DANNY *and* HELEN. HELEN *is as far from anyone's idea of an aunt as one can get.*

She's no more beautiful than JENNY, *but she's dressed both appropriately and spectacularly, in early-'60s, pre-hippy Bohemian gear. She turns heads in a way that* JENNY *is not yet able to.* DANNY, *too, is attractive, but soberly so.* DAVID *and* JENNY *are, in a way, paler, less striking versions of these two.*

DAVID

Hello, hello. Are we late?

HELEN

No, I thought we were going to miss the beginning, and then it wouldn't be worth going in, and we could all go off dancing or something.

DANNY

Helen is one of the more reluctant members
of tonight's audience.

JENNY *and* DAVID *laugh politely.*

DAVID

Jenny, these are my friends Helen and Danny.

JENNY *shakes hands with the two of them. They both
give her fascinated and clearly appraising looks. They
have heard about her.*

Shall we?

They walk into the hall.

18 INTERIOR: ST JOHN'S, SMITH
SQUARE – NIGHT

It's a beautiful hall – JENNY *is dazzled by the surroundings and the company. She's particularly bowled over by*
HELEN.

*The girls walk over to the cloakroom where they join the
queue. Almost involuntarily,* JENNY *touches the sleeve of*
HELEN'S *fur jacket. She stops herself.* HELEN *notices.*

JENNY
Sorry.

HELEN
(*amused*)
That's all right. It's nice, isn't it?

JENNY

It's beautiful. Where did you get it from?

HELEN

Oh, I don't know, Chelsea somewhere.

HELEN *looks at* JENNY'S *outfit, her frumpy 'smart' dress, apparently wanting to return the compliment.*

(*nodding at the dress*)
This is . . . Well, it's good for this sort of concert, isn't it?

JENNY

(*quietly*)
Thank you.

HELEN *is now at the front of the queue and hands her coat over imperiously.*

HELEN

We should go shopping together one day, if you want.

She takes a ticket from the cloakroom lady.

JENNY

That would be nice. But Chelsea . . . *C'est beaucoup trop cher pour moi.*

They stare at each other. HELEN *is bewildered,* JENNY *embarrassed.*

HELEN

Sorry?

JENNY

I just said . . . It's too expensive for me.

HELEN

No you didn't. You said something completely different.

JENNY

I just . . . Well, I said it in French.

HELEN

In French? Why?

JENNY *feels humiliated; she is yet to realise what we can see – that* HELEN *is simply very dim.*

JENNY

I don't know.

JENNY *looks away.* HELEN *stares at her. The performance bell rings, and they make their way back to the men.*

To JENNY'S *surprise and pleasure,* HELEN *links arms with her as they walk.*

HELEN

Well, Chelsea's too expensive for me, too, really. But we don't have to worry about that. If you want something in Chelsea, get David to take you shopping.

JENNY

Why would David want to take me shopping?

HELEN *makes a knowing face.*

19 INTERIOR: ST JOHN'S, SMITH SQUARE – NIGHT

DAVID, JENNY, DANNY *and* HELEN *in a row in the middle of the auditorium, watching the stage and listening to the music.* JENNY *can't concentrate – she's too excited by the occasion and the company.* JENNY *sneaks a glance at* HELEN, *who stares straight ahead, unblinking and enigmatic.* DAVID *is smiling, as if he's trying to communicate enjoyment;* DANNY'S *eyes flicker across the stage – he understands the music, its component parts, which musicians are contributing what.* JENNY *takes it all in.*

20 EXTERIOR: ST JOHN'S, SMITH SQUARE – NIGHT

JENNY, DAVID, DANNY *and* HELEN *emerge with the other concert-goers.*

> DAVID
>
> I booked a table at Juliette's. Will that kill the mood, do you think?

> HELEN
>
> Oh, I do hope so.

The others laugh.

> I always think I'm going to my own funeral when I listen to classical music. (*tentatively*) That was classical, wasn't it?

DANNY

Yes. Very classical. As classical as you can get.

HELEN *looks pleased.*

DAVID

Juliette's it is, then. Heaven forbid that we should end the evening reflecting on our own mortality.

JENNY *smiles in delight. She's never met people like this.*

21   INTERIOR: JULIETTE'S – NIGHT

A singer in the Julie London mould is singing while cigarette girls and glamorous waitresses patrol the tables. JENNY *is sitting with the others at a table in the club, eating and talking. She looks about twelve, but she's thrilled to be there. We know now that her life can never be the same again, and there will be no going back to fish-paste sandwiches with pimply* GRAHAM.

DANNY

(*mid-conversation*)
. . . Miles Davis, Sartre, extraordinary woman, Greco. (*aside*) Just like you, Helen.

DAVID

What about Chante Françoise Sagan? Have you heard that one?

JENNY *shakes her head. Her eyes are wide – she's clearly awestruck.* DAVID *offers her a cigarette – a Gitane – which she takes. He lights it for her while she's listening.*

DANNY
Oh, it's wonderful.

JENNY
I've only got . . . Well, I think it's just called 'Juliette Greco'. The one with the eyes on the sleeve. I saved up and got my French conversation teacher to bring it back after Christmas.

HELEN
You've got a French conversation teacher?

JENNY
Yes.

HELEN
Is that why you suddenly speak French for no reason?

DAVID
(*to* JENNY)
Have you never heard her sing?

JENNY *shakes her head again and smiles. Where would she have seen Juliette Greco?* DANNY, *meanwhile, is baffled. Who hasn't seen Juliette Greco?*

She's marvellous.

DANNY

You should see her in Paris, though, not here.
David will take you.

DAVID

I'd love to. You'd fit right in.

HELEN

(*sympathetically*)
Better than here, really.

DAVID

It's wonderful to find a young person who
wants to know things. There's so much I want
you to see.

HELEN *and* DANNY *exchange glances and they all sip
their drinks pensively, possibly to allow time for the
double-entendre to disappear into the smoke.*

Are you still all right to come and have a look
at that Pembroke Villas place with me on
Friday, Danny?

DANNY

Oh. No. Can't do it. There's a Burne-Jones
coming up at Christie's on Friday. Desperate
to get my hands on it.

JENNY

(*laughing in disbelief*)
You're thinking of buying a Burne-Jones? A
real one?

DANNY

I just have a feeling that the Pre-Raphaelites are going to take off.

JENNY

I love the Pre-Raphaelites.

DAVID

(*excited by her education*)
Do you?

JENNY

Yes, of course. Rossetti and Burne-Jones, anyway. Not Holman Hunt, so much. He's so garish.

DANNY *looks at her. There's clearly more to this school-girl than he thought.*

DAVID

Absolutely! Why don't we all go to the auction together?

JENNY

An auction. Gosh. How exciting.

DANNY

Next Friday morning.

JENNY

(*crestfallen*)
Oh. Friday.

DANNY

You're busy?

JENNY

Well. Yes.

She doesn't want to explain why.

DANNY

Tant pis. Quel dommage . . .

HELEN *looks at him aghast. Why has he started speaking French?*

DAVID

Are you sure you're busy?

JENNY *hesitates.*

JENNY

No. I'm sure I could . . . re-arrange. That would be lovely.

The nightclub singer begins another song, 'Wrapped Around Your Little Finger'. DANNY *and* HELEN *know this one and sing romantically along with one another.* JENNY *watches them entranced, then turns and smiles at* DAVID.

22   INTERIOR: JENNY'S HOUSE – NIGHT

JENNY *lets herself quietly into the house. The hallway is dark, but she can hear noises from the kitchen. She pokes*

her head round the corner and sees her mother doing the
washing-up.

JENNY

What are you doing?

MARJORIE

I can't get this casserole dish clean. We had
hot-pot tonight, and it's all burnt round . . .

JENNY

It's twenty-five to twelve. We finish tea at
seven.

MARJORIE

I know what time it is. How was your
evening?

JENNY

Best night of my life.

JENNY *looks at her. She doesn't seem to have heard what*
JENNY *has just said.*

Goodnight, Mum.

MARJORIE *carries on scrubbing, turning to look at*
JENNY *as she leaves the kitchen.*

23   INTERIOR: CLASSROOM – DAY

JENNY, HATTIE *and* TINA *are sitting on their desks,*
waiting for the start of a lesson. Nine or ten classmates

are scattered round the room, talking distractedly, but
JENNY'S *group is much more animated:* TINA *and*
HATTIE *are leaning forward, listening to* JENNY, *their
eyes bright. They are clearly awestruck by* JENNY'S *tales
of the outside world.*

JENNY

I think there were two violins, one cello, two
violas, a harp . . .

TINA

(*to* HATTIE)
I don't want to know about Ravel. I want to
know what else was on the programme.

Laughter.

JENNY

There was nothing like that. He was the
perfect gentleman. He just said he wanted to
take me places and show me things.

HATTIE/TINA

Things! Plural! Oh my Gawd!

More laughter. MISS STUBBS *enters and picks up on the
excitement of* JENNY'S *coterie.*

MISS STUBBS

I knew that in the end *Jane Eyre* would work
its magic upon you. I'm assuming that's what
you're all so animated about.

The students start to sit down at desks in a more conventional arrangement.

JENNY

Of course.

TINA

Jane Eyre and Jenny's new boyfriend.

JENNY

He's not my new boyfriend. God.

TINA

That's true. He's more of a man-friend, actually.

HATTIE

He's got a sports car, Miss Stubbs. It's maroon.

MISS STUBBS

Ah. So we could call him a Mr Rochester figure.

TINA

I think he must be as blind as Mr Rochester.

Laughter. JENNY *pulls a face at her.*

MISS STUBBS

You may or may not have noticed, I'm trying to steer the subject away from Jenny's lurid love-life and towards the matter in hand.

She starts to hand out essays.

> And it's quite clear on this evidence that
> most of you know far too much about the
> former, and next to nothing about the latter.
> Reluctantly I have to admit that Jenny is
> clearly an expert on both. Excellent as always,
> Jenny.

MISS STUBBS *slaps an essay down on* JENNY'S *desk. We
can see that it's marked 'A+'.*

24 EXTERIOR: DAVID'S CAR – DAY

DAVID *leaning against his Bristol, waiting.*

25 EXTERIOR: SCHOOL – DAY

We see JENNY *rush out of the school entrance, stuffing
her school uniform into her bag and trying to avoid being
noticed. She walks up to* DAVID, *parked on the opposite
side of the street.*

> DAVID
> Hello.

> JENNY
> (*laughing*)
> Hello.

DAVID *and* JENNY *hurry into the hall where the auction is taking place.*

At the back, DANNY *is intent on a catalogue and* HELEN *is gazing dreamily into space, as* DAVID *and* JENNY *make their way through the auction room. The* AUCTIONEER *burbles on in the background.*

> DANNY
>
> You're late.

JENNY *is in awe of the surroundings. The* AUCTIONEER *clears his throat.*

> AUCTIONEER
>
> We now turn to Lot 41, *The Tree of Forgiveness*, by Sir Edward Burne-Jones. This is a rare opportunity to purchase a key work of the Pre-Raphaelite movement. Who will start me off at one hundred guineas?

JENNY *glances at* DANNY. *He makes no move at this price. Neither does anyone else. He's poised and listening hard.*

> Fifty guineas? . . . Twenty guineas?

A middle-aged lady, the epitome of the middle-aged contemporary Sloane – twin-set, pearls and a lot of face powder – raises her hand.

> Thank you, madam. Forty?

A man raises his hand.

Thank you, sir. Do I hear sixty?

The middle-aged Sloane nods.

Eighty guineas? Thank you. Any more, sir?
One hundred guineas . . .

DANNY *continues to sit there.* JENNY *is confused. The
middle-aged lady bids a hundred.* DAVID, *standing next
to* DANNY, *whispers something to him.* DANNY *nods.*

DAVID
(*whispers to* JENNY)
Your turn.

JENNY *looks at him.*

JENNY
(*whispers*)
What?

AUCTIONEER
Any further bids?

DAVID
(*whispers*)
Your turn.

AUCTIONEER
Any more?

DAVID
Quick!

JENNY *raises her hand high, just as she'd do at school.*

AUCTIONEER

One hundred and twenty guineas from the very eager new bidder.

People look round and smile when they see who has come in. JENNY *blushes, but stares fixedly ahead.*

One hundred and forty, madam? Thank you.

JENNY *looks at* DAVID, *who nods.*

One hundred and sixty guineas.

JENNY *gestures more economically.*

One eighty? Thank you, madam. Two hundred . . .

JENNY *is almost insouciant this time.*

Two hundred and twenty? Another one, madam?

The middle-aged lady shakes her head and purses her lips. The AUCTIONEER *looks round the room for any last-minute bidders, then:*

Sold for two hundred guineas. Thank you.

He brings down the gavel, and a murmur goes round the room. JENNY *is excited and giggly.* DAVID *pats her on the back.*

Your name, please?

JENNY *looks at* DANNY, *then back to the auctioneer.*

JENNY
(*too loudly*)
Mellor.

Murmurs from the room. The auctioneer moves on to the next Lot, while DAVID *and* DANNY *turn to* JENNY.

> DANNY
>
> Thank you. Couldn't possibly have bought it without you.

JENNY *beams. She's thrilled.*

27 EXTERIOR: LONDON STREET – DAY

The Bristol pulls into a smart Regency terrace. We hear their conversation from the car.

> DANNY (*out of sight*)
>
> A couple of years ago you could pick one of them up for fifty quid, you know. Nobody was interested.

> JENNY (*out of sight*)
>
> I would have been *so* interested.

28 INTERIOR: DANNY'S FLAT – DAY

A beautiful, large, airy sitting room inside the terrace apartment. The flat is unusually and tastefully decorated, opulent and indicative of Bohemian good taste. JENNY *is sipping a glass of white wine and walking around the room enthralled, looking at* DANNY'S *collection.*

Suddenly JENNY *sees a cello in the corner of the room – a good one.*

JENNY

That's not a Lockey-Hill!

DANNY

There aren't many people who come in here
and say that.

HELEN

Certainly not me.

JENNY

It's beautiful. Do you play?

DANNY

I used to. I vowed to myself that one day I'd
own one of these. And now that I do own
one, I never touch the bugger. It's vulgar to
put it on show, really.

HELEN

Give it to Jenny.

DANNY

That would be even more vulgar.

DAVID

Play for us, Jenny.

JENNY

Gosh, no. One day. When I'm good enough.

DAVID

She's good enough now.

JENNY

Oh, David. You've never seen me play.

DAVID

I shall come to hear you in Oxford, when you get there.

DANNY

We should all go and spend a weekend in Oxford. Straw boaters –

HELEN

(*cutting in*)
Boats!

DANNY

– punting, cream teas, antiquarian book-shops . . . Bit of business, if we can find it. What about next weekend?

DAVID/HELEN

Yes!

JENNY

I wouldn't be allowed to do that.

They all look at her.

DAVID

I'll talk to them.

JENNY *hoots with derision.*

JENNY

You're going to ask my father if you can take me away for the weekend? He'd have you arrested.

DAVID

We'll see.

JENNY

I'll bet you you can't.

DAVID

How much?

DANNY

(*amused*)

I'd be careful, if I were you, Jenny. You don't know who you're dealing with.

JENNY

Half-a-crown.

DAVID

You're on.

INTERIOR/EXTERIOR: DAVID'S CAR/
DILAPIDATED HOUSE – DAY

JENNY *and* DAVID *are driving along a North Kensington street.*

> JENNY
>
> How do you know Danny?

DAVID *is distracted. He's driving slowly, apparently looking for an address.*

> DAVID
>
> Oh, you know. We kept bumping into each other, and we became pals, and we've ended up doing a bit of business together, when it suits us.
>
> JENNY
>
> What kind of business?
>
> DAVID
>
> Property. A bit of art dealing. Some buying and selling. This and that . . .

He stops the car.

> Right. I'll just be two ticks.

He gets out of the car, and JENNY *watches him as he crosses the road. Outside a dilapidated house covered in scaffolding stands a large West Indian family – mother, father, three or four small children and a dog. They are surrounded by what appears to be all their worldly goods.*

DAVID *squats down on his haunches, talks to the kids, tousles the hair of the smallest. Then he takes out a bunch of keys and ushers the family down the path. He unlocks the door and leads them inside.*

In an upper window of the house, we see an old lady peering down anxiously.

30 EXTERIOR: STREET/DILAPIDATED HOUSE – DAY

DAVID *emerges from the house, jangling his keys.*

31 INTERIOR: DAVID'S CAR – DAY

JENNY *opens the glove compartment where* DAVID *keeps his cigarettes, takes out the packet, removes and lights one for herself.* DAVID *gets in.*

> DAVID
> Sorry about that.

> JENNY
> How do you know those . . . Negro people?

> DAVID
> They're clients.

> JENNY
> Clients?

DAVID

Schwarzers have to live somewhere. It's not as if they can rent off their own kind, is it?

He starts the car and drives off.

32   INTERIOR: CLASSROOM/LATIN – DAY

JENNY *is in her Latin class, waiting for the lesson to begin.* TINA *and* HATTIE *aren't with her, and she sits on her own – the atmosphere of the class is very different from* MISS STUBBS' *English lessons. The girls are different, more serious, less fun, and the atmosphere is more sombre. The teacher,* MRS WILSON, *is older, plainer, stricter. She holds some papers.*

MRS WILSON

Test results for the Virgil translation. We will start from the bottom . . . Patricia.

JENNY *puffs out her cheeks. She's not last.*

Absent. Margaret. 48 per cent. Jenny . . .

JENNY *winces.*

52 per cent. That would just about scrape a pass in the exam proper. Not good enough for Oxford candidates.

33   INTERIOR/EXTERIOR: JENNY'S HOUSE – DAY

JENNY *and her mother are sitting on the sofa, staring into space, clearly upset. On the coffee table in front of them is the test, covered in red ink.*

JACK *enters, back from work. He's wearing a suit and carrying a battered briefcase. He looks at them, and then notices the essay on the table.*

JACK
It's her Latin, isn't it?

MARJORIE
Everyone's doing their best, Jack.

JACK
But what if everyone's best isn't good enough? What do we do then?

JENNY
We don't go to Oxford. Any of us.
Not even you, Dad.

JACK
Perhaps the whole thing's a waste of time and money anyway.

MARJORIE
You don't mean that.

JACK

Well, what's she going to do with an English degree? If she's going to spend three years playing that bloody cello and talking in French to a bunch of beatniks, then I'm just throwing good money after bad. I suppose she might meet a nice lawyer. But she could do that at a dinner dance tomorrow.

JENNY

Oh, because that's the point of an Oxford education, isn't it, Dad? It's the expensive alternative to a dinner dance.

MARJORIE

What about private tuition?

JACK

Is anyone listening to me? How much is that going to cost me?

MARJORIE

Five shillings an hour. Maybe a little more for A-level.

JACK

Five bob! We spend five bob here and five bob there, next thing you know it's our savings down the drain.

MARJORIE

And what else are we spending five bob on?
What else are we spending sixpence on?

JACK

Oh, nothing. (*He gestures round the room.*) All
of this is free. That vase was free.

MARJORIE

It was, actually. It was a present from Auntie Vi.

JACK

That chair was free. The sofa. We don't have
to pay for anything. That's the beauty of life,
Jenny. Everything's free. Grows on trees.
Wonderful, isn't it? (*He warms to his theme
and grows progressively more berserk.*) We've got
a lovely Oxford tree in the garden, lucky for
you, so that's Oxford taken care of. And a
whole orchard of school trees, so that's all
free. I'm sure there are some private tuition
trees out there. I'll go and have a look.

He stands up.

MARJORIE

Jack . . .

JACK

No, no, won't take me a minute. I think I saw
some out the front, right next to the pocket
money tree. I'll just nip out and check, see

that they're doing all right. Don't want anyone climbing over the wall and scrumping, do we? And you never know. Maybe there'll be a man with deep pockets growing out there. Because God knows we need to find you one.

He leaves the room, apparently to look in the front garden for the mythical trees.

34 EXTERIOR: STREET/COFFEE BAR – DAY

JENNY, HATTIE *and* TINA *are walking back from school.*

TINA
You can always go to secretarial college with Hattie.

JENNY
(*sarcastic*)
Oh, thanks.

HATTIE
Charming!

JENNY
Oh, God, no.

HATTIE *and* TINA *follow* JENNY'S *eyes, and they see* GRAHAM *coming towards them pushing his bike, red-faced, trousers tucked into socks.*

GRAHAM

Hello.

JENNY

Hello, Graham.

GRAHAM

I haven't seen you in ages . . . It went a bit
wrong, didn't it? The tea-party, I mean. Was
it because of the year off thing?

JENNY

No. I just have so much work to do if I'm
going to get the grades I need.

TINA

Yes. She doesn't have time for boys.

HATTIE *and* TINA *try to suppress giggles.* GRAHAM
turns an even brighter shade of red. HATTIE *and* TINA
enter the coffee bar. JENNY *feels sorry for him, is on the
verge of inviting him to join them . . . And changes her
mind.*

JENNY

(*quickly*)
Bye, Graham.

She follows the girls inside.

GRAHAM

Bye.

35 INTERIOR: JENNY'S BEDROOM/ UPPER HALLWAY – NIGHT

JENNY *is deep in her schoolwork. She has a Latin vocabulary propped open on the window ledge. She looks at it, walks away, mutters to herself, attempting to memorise. Her concentration is broken by a sudden gale of laughter from downstairs.*

36 INTERIOR: JENNY'S HALLWAY – NIGHT

She stands outside the living room for a moment, listening. She hears a man's voice that does not belong to her father, and then more laughter from her father and mother.

37 INTERIOR: JENNY'S HOUSE – NIGHT

DAVID *is in the middle of demonstrating his ability to mimic all of the Goons.* JACK *and* MARJORIE *are laughing so hard that they can hardly see – they certainly miss* JENNY'S *entrance.*

> JENNY
> (*curious*)
> Hello.

JACK

Jenny, David does the most fantastic
Bluebottle.

JENNY

(*incredulous*)
You came to see my parents?

JACK

Why is that so hard to imagine?

JENNY *spies an open bottle of wine on the coffee table.*

JENNY

Why are you drinking? It's not Christmas!

JACK

Ah, well, there's a lot you don't know about
us, young lady. We had a life before you came
along.

JENNY

Yes, that's true. I'm only going on what I've
seen for the last sixteen years.

MARJORIE

I'm trying to think what you missed. Nothing
much comes to mind.

JENNY

Anyway. I've got a huge pile of Latin translation to do.

JACK

You didn't tell us David went to Oxford.

JENNY *looks at* DAVID, *who stares back at her straight-faced.*

JENNY

No. I didn't.

DAVID

For all the good it did me.

MARJORIE

Isn't that funny?

JENNY

Extraordinary.

DAVID

I was just telling Jack that I'm going back next weekend. I go and visit my old English professor every now and again.

JACK

That's what you need, Jenny. Someone on the inside track. It's not always what you know, is it, David?

DAVID

Too true. Have you ever come across Clive Lewis?

JENNY

Dad has never come across anyone.

DAVID

He wrote a children's book called *The Lion, the Witch and the Wardrobe* that did very well, I believe.

MARJORIE

C. S. Lewis? That's the Clive you're talking about?

DAVID

Well, to us he was the old codger who taught Medieval literature. But I came to know him very well. We just . . . got along, you know?

Everyone murmurs their comprehension.

MARJORIE

Jenny used to devour those books.

JENNY

I'd love to meet him.

There is a pause. JACK *and* MARJORIE *look at the floor. Somehow,* DAVID *has manoeuvred a situation where, effectively, he is the one being asked.*

DAVID

I'm sorry. Am I being slow on the uptake? Would Jenny like to come at the weekend?

JACK

Oh, not this weekend. Sometime, perhaps, yes.

JENNY

How often do you see him?

DAVID

Not very often. Every couple of years. Maybe next time?

JENNY

(*disappointed*)
Oh.

JACK

(*dubiously*)
Well, I suppose . . . Would she have to stay the night?

DAVID

I wouldn't recommend driving home after one of those Oxford dinners.

JACK *chuckles knowingly.*

Clive could get her a room at the college. It's easy enough.

MARJORIE

Seems like too good an opportunity to pass up.

JACK

It wouldn't be a bother to you, would it,
David?

JACK, MARJORIE and JENNY all beam.

38   INTERIOR: DANNY'S FLAT – DAY

DAVID and DANNY are waiting for the girls to get ready.
DANNY is sitting sprawled in an armchair; DAVID is
pacing up and down.

DAVID

Come on!

39   INTERIOR: HELEN'S BEDROOM – DAY

An ornate four-poster bed occupies most of the space in
the room. HELEN is doing something to JENNY, but we
can't see what.

HELEN

Just putting a few things in a bag. Don't worry!

40   INTERIOR: DANNY'S FLAT – DAY

DAVID and DANNY still waiting.

DAVID

Come on!

41   INTERIOR: HELEN'S BEDROOM – DAY

HELEN

We're nearly ready! Be there in two ticks.

42   INTERIOR: DANNY'S FLAT – DAY

DAVID

How can they only be nearly ready?

DANNY

I wouldn't be surprised if three of them came
out of there. That's the only explantion.
They're making themselves a friend.
LADIES! Come on, let's go.

43   INTERIOR: HELEN'S BEDROOM – DAY

JENNY *is wearing a floaty print dress that she has
borrowed from* HELEN, *and there are lots of other beautiful clothes strewn about the place.* JENNY *is sitting at the
dressing table, being made up by* HELEN. JENNY *looks
three or four years older, more sophisticated . . . more like*
HELEN. *She can't believe it. She looks in the mirror, and
for a moment, she forgets to breathe.*

HELEN

There. You should keep that one if you
want it. One can only wear so many every
day.

JENNY *emerges from her reverie.*

JENNY
(*thrilled*)
Thank you.

HELEN

What about tonight? Have you got a pretty
enough nightie?

JENNY

Won't I be sharing a room with you?

HELEN *looks momentarily mystified.*

HELEN

Oh, you haven't slept with him yet?

JENNY
No.

HELEN
Good for you.

JENNY
Really? Do you think so?

HELEN

You're only sixteen. And you don't want to get preggers, do you?

JENNY

No. I wouldn't let that happen. I want to wait until I'm seventeen. On my seventeenth birthday, hopefully.

HELEN

With David?

JENNY *pauses.*

JENNY

Well . . . Golly. It will be with David, won't it?

HELEN

If that's what you want. Anyway. I'll find you a nightie.

JENNY *stares at herself in the mirror again.*

44 INTERIOR: DANNY'S FLAT – DAY

The girls emerge. Both men are entranced by JENNY'S *transformation.* DAVID *can't take his eyes off her.*

DANNY

(*thoughtful*)
Shall, we, ah . . . Make a move?

He gets to his feet.

45 INTERIOR/EXTERIOR: DAVID'S CAR/ COUNTRY ROAD – DAY

The Bristol on the country road to Oxford. We can hear voices in the car singing a reprise of 'Wrapped around Your Little Finger'.

46 INTERIOR/EXTERIOR: DAVID'S CAR, OXFORD – DAY

The Bristol drives through Oxford. JENNY *catches a quick glimpse of a dreaming spire.*

JENNY

Can we get out and have a look around?

DAVID

Maybe later. There are a couple of things we have to do.

DANNY

Imagine spending three years here.

HELEN

I know.

She shudders, as if someone has walked over her grave.

HELEN and DANNY, JENNY *and* DAVID *are standing in
a quiet, old-fashioned pub. A group of students enter, all
carrying musical instruments. They stand at the bar,
waiting to be served.* JENNY *stares at them with longing –
she wants to be one of them.* HELEN, *meanwhile, stares at
them as if they were aliens.*

> HELEN
>
> (*sotto voce*)
> Why are university girls so strange-looking?

HELEN'S *right. The girls in the group are all bespectacled
and frumpy. The others laugh.*

> They can't all have started off that way, can
> they? I mean most girls aren't ugly, but most
> girl students seem to be. So there must be
> something about these places that makes you
> fat, or spotty, or short-sighted.

> DAVID
>
> Well, if you look at it like that . . . I mean,
> that's proper scientific analysis. And you can't
> argue with science.

HELEN *looks pleased.*

> HELEN
>
> I still don't quite understand what you want
> to do when you get here.

JENNY

I want to read English.

HELEN

Books?

JENNY

Sorry?

HELEN

You want to read English *books*?

JENNY

Reading English is just another way of
saying . . .

DANNY

Don't worry, Jenny. You're wasting your
breath.

DAVID

Tomorrow we'll get more of a feel for the
place.

DANNY

Absolutely. This would be a good place to do
a little business.

DAVID *catches* JENNY'S *eye. This isn't what he meant by
'getting a feel for the place'.*

All those little old ladies wandering around . . .
This place is rife with stats.

JENNY

Please explain what stats are. You're always
going on about them.

DAVID

It isn't very interesting.

JENNY

But you two are interested.

DAVID

That's because we're not very interesting,
either.

HELEN

Oh, no, they're not really.

DANNY

It's true. That's why we need you here. To
save us from ourselves.

DAVID

(*laying it on with a trowel*)
Yes, to put some intelligence and culture into
our brutal lives.

DANNY

Sing to us, sing to us.

JENNY

Please don't make me sing to you.

DAVID

Please don't make us talk about work.

JENNY *and* HELEN *laugh.*

CUT TO:

Later. They're standing by the pub fireplace. DAVID *has a pen in his hand, and he's holding a book –* The Lion, the Witch and the Wardrobe.

DAVID

Now. Is he Clive, do you think? Or C. S.?

HELEN

I'm confused now. I thought you'd made him up?

DANNY

(*attempting, briefly, to be patient*)
No, we . . . Never mind.

DAVID *walks over to the nearest table and writes in the book.*

DAVID

There.

He stands up, hands the book to Jenny.

JENNY

(*reads*)
'To dear Jenny.
With the pleasure of meeting you. Come and see me again soon. Clive.'

HELEN

Dirty old man.

48 INTERIOR: B & B BEDROOM – NIGHT

A rather grotty and certainly unromantic B & B bedroom – so unromantic, in fact, that it even has the same fusty curtains from JENNY'S *sitting room.* DAVID *is in bed, his hands behind his head, waiting for* JENNY. *As far as we can tell – he's wrapped up in the sheets quite tightly – he's in his underwear. The bedroom is lit unromantically by the 40-watt overhead light.* JENNY *comes into the room wearing one of* HELEN'S *nightdresses, a glamorous satiny item quite inappropriate for the occasion or the surroundings. She looks nervous.*

JENNY

We've got these exact same curtains at home.

DAVID

Let's not talk about curtains. You look beautiful.

JENNY *was about to get into bed, but his tone makes her pause at the edge of the bed.*

JENNY

There's something you should know, David. I'm a virgin. And I want to stay that way until I'm seventeen.

DAVID

I think that's good. I think that's right. We can still be romantic, though, can't we?

JENNY

Well, yes. Of course we can. As long as it's not actually . . .

DAVID

Minnie . . .

JENNY

Is that me?

DAVID

Yes. You're my Minnie Mouse, and I'm your bubbalub.

JENNY

OK. If that's what you want to do . . .

DAVID

Minnie.

JENNY

Yes, David?

DAVID

(*prompting*)
Bubbalub . . .

JENNY

Bubbalub?

DAVID

May I have a look? Just a peek?

His eyes stray to her breasts. JENNY *stares at him.*

JENNY

You just want to *see* them?

JENNY, *awkwardly, looks down at her nightgown, then one by one pulls the straps down. It fall from her shoulders.*

DAVID *stands up and lovingly lifts the straps back up.*

DAVID

Thank you.

He smiles at her. Relieved, she smiles back. He puts his arms around her and they embrace.

49 INTERIOR/EXTERIOR: DAVID'S CAR/ COTTAGE – DAY

The Bristol, containing DAVID *and* JENNY *in the front seats and* DANNY *and* HELEN *in the back, passing through a pretty Oxfordshire village.*

DAVID

I think there's a house for sale around here.

DANNY

Really?

The Bristol pulls up outside a country cottage with a 'FOR SALE' sign outside.

50   INTERIOR: DAVID'S CAR – DAY

DAVID

Might be worth a look.

51   INTERIOR/EXTERIOR: DAVID'S CAR/
      COTTAGE – DAY

DAVID, DANNY *and* JENNY *get out of the car, and* JENNY *heads after* DAVID *and* DANNY *towards the house.* HELEN *stays in the car.*

HELEN
(*calling from the window*)
Jenny!

JENNY *turns around.*

JENNY

Aren't you coming?

HELEN

We don't go in.

JENNY

What are you talking about?

DANNY

Why don't you get a nice cup of tea somewhere? Helen will look after you.

JENNY *is mystified.*

JENNY

I don't need looking after, thank you very
much. David!

DAVID *ignores her and walks off arm in arm with* DANNY.

DANNY

I'm not going to tell you a second time. Run
along.

52   EXTERIOR: COTTAGE – DAY

HELEN *and* JENNY *walking around the village waiting
for the boys.* HELEN *is blithe, chatty;* JENNY *has a face
like thunder.*

HELEN

They won't be long. Either way.

JENNY

'Either way'?

HELEN

Sometimes they find something, and sometimes they don't. And when they do find
something, we often have to leave quite
quickly. They can be a bit naughty sometimes.

JENNY *stares at* HELEN. *She's beginning to realise who
she is dealing with.*

Anyway, it's nice to have company.
I'm usually outside on my own.

53   EXTERIOR: CAR/COTTAGE – DAY

DAVID *and* DANNY *hurry out of the cottage, something
under* DANNY'S *coat.* DAVID *rushes towards the car, past*
JENNY *playing catch with a small child.*

DAVID

Come on. (*to Helen, lounging by the car*)
Helen!

DAVID *and* HELEN *get in,* DANNY *opens the door while*
JENNY *hesitates.*

DANNY

(*calling*)
You can stand there if you like.
But I wouldn't recommend it.

JENNY *puts a spurt on, catches up and jumps in.*

54   INTERIOR/EXTERIOR: DAVID'S CAR/ NEW COUNTRY ROAD – DAY

An old picture of some kind is wedged between HELEN *and* JENNY *on the backseat.* JENNY, *furious, is staring out of the window.* HELEN *attempts to peer around the partition, but settles for a wave.*

> HELEN
> Coo-ee. Jenny.

JENNY *doesn't respond. They continue driving in silence.*

55   EXTERIOR: DANNY'S FLAT – DAY

The Bristol pulls up outside DANNY'S *Regency terrace. They all get out of the car and pull out their weekend cases.*

> DANNY
> Who's coming up for a drink?

> HELEN
> Me!

> JENNY
> (*still furious*)
> No, you go. I'll make my own way home.

JENNY *starts up the road.* DAVID *walks briskly after her.*

> DAVID
> Jenny!

He catches up with her in the street.

It's an old map. A Speed. The poor dear
didn't even know what it was. What a waste!
It shouldn't spend its life on a wall in wher-
ever the hell we were. It should be with us.
We know how to look after it properly. We
liberated it.

JENNY *snorts derisively.*

JENNY

Liberated! That's one word for it.

DAVID

(*quickly and passionately*)
Don't be bourgeois, Jenny. You're better than
that. You drink everything I put in front of
you down in one, then you slam your glass
down on the bar and ask for more. It's wonderful. We're not clever like you, so we have
to be clever in other ways, because if we
weren't, there would be no fun. We have to be
clever with maps, and . . . and . . . You want to
know what stats are? Stats are old ladies who
are scared of coloured people. So we move
the coloureds in and the old ladies move out
and I buy their flats cheap. That's what I do.
So now you know.

JENNY *nods reluctantly.*

And if you don't like it, I'll understand, and
you can go back to Twickenham and listen to

the Home Service and do your Latin homework. But these weekends, and the restaurants and the concerts . . . They don't grow on
trees.

JENNY *looks at him, startled. Trees again?*

This is who we are, Jenny.

He turns to face her and holds out his hand. On JENNY:
is she in or out? JENNY *takes his hand.* DAVID *pulls her
towards him, holds her around the waist and begins to
dance with her. From the apartment balcony,* HELEN
and DANNY *watch, laughing.*

56   INTERIOR/EXTERIOR: DAVID'S CAR/ JENNY'S HOUSE – NIGHT

DAVID *pulls up in the Bristol outside* JENNY'S *house,
and they sit in the dark for a little while.*

DAVID

I suppose you have homework to do.

JENNY

You have no idea how boring everything was
before I met you. Action is character, our
English teacher says. I think it means that if we
never did anything, we wouldn't be anybody.
And I never did anything before I met you. And
sometimes I think no one's ever done anything
in this stupid country, apart from you.

They look at each other. DAVID *smiles. He is clearly smitten. He moves towards her. He wants to kiss her, but he doesn't want to frighten her – in the end,* JENNY *makes it easy for him and moves towards him. They kiss gently and tenderly.* JENNY *breaks it off, gets out of the car,* DAVID *hands her her suitcase and she goes inside while he watches.*

57   INTERIOR: JENNY'S HOUSE – NIGHT

JACK, *at the kitchen table, is examining* JENNY'S *copy of* The Lion, the Witch and the Wardrobe.

> JACK
> Look at this, Marjorie.

He hands it to her. She examines it reverently.

> MARJORIE
> 'Clive' . . . Lucky girl.

> JACK
> Never a dull moment with David, eh? Bit different from that young man you brought home for tea, isn't he?

> MARJORIE
> David's a lot older than Graham.

> JACK
> Graham could live to be two hundred years

old and still wouldn't be swanning around with famous authors. Hasn't got it in him.

JENNY

Graham might *become* a famous author, for all you know.

JACK

Becoming one isn't the same as knowing one . . . That shows you're well connected. A very impressive young man, your David.

MARJORIE.

I must admit life's a little brighter with him around.

JENNY *smiles to herself.*

58 EXTERIOR: PARK – DAY

A group of girls cross-country running. JENNY *and her friends are at the back of the group, and the* GYM TEACHER, *jogging backwards, gesticulates at them to get a move on.*

GYM TEACHER

Come on, girls. Get a move on.

They put on enough of a spurt to satisfy her, and then immediately stop when the teacher is no longer watching. Seeing a large tree, they loiter. From somewhere under a skirt, JENNY *produces a packet of exotic-looking cigarettes and offers them around.*

HATTIE

What the hell are those?

JENNY

Russian Sobranies.

HATTIE *and* TINA *make snooty faces.* JENNY *takes a cigarette. The others follow suit.* JENNY *lights them, and they all grimace. The contrast between the sophisticated cigarettes, and the unsophisticated smokers and context is pronounced.*

HATTIE

Where did they come from?

TINA

She probably bought them from the Savoy, or Claridge's, or the opera, or some fancy night-club. Who knows, with Jenny.

JENNY

Paris. You can't buy them here.

TINA

(*suddenly looking at her suspiciously*)
You never bought them yourself?

JENNY

(*mimicking* TINA'S *grammar cruelly*)
No. I never.

TINA

Shut up, you stuck-up cow.

JENNY

But I'll bring you some back, if you want.

TINA

You're joking.

JENNY

Non.

HATTIE

He's taking you to Paris?

JENNY
(*smiling smugly*)
Oui.

HATTIE

This term?

JENNY

Peut-être.

TINA

Isn't it your birthday next Thursday?

JENNY

Might be.

The two friends shriek and jump up and down.

HATTIE

Oh, my God! Your birthday!

TINA

I would not like to be you. All those suppers you've had off him. Ouch.

JENNY

You've such a Victorian attitude to sex, you two.

TINA

Oh, sorry, Dr Kinsey. We're not all as experienced as you. I mean, you've done it . . . (*She counts on her fingers*) I make it never! Can that be right?

HATTIE

But your parents wouldn't let you swan off like that, would they?

JENNY

We haven't told them yet. But David will come up with some story. He usually does.

TINA

Yeah, I've noticed that.

Laughter. JENNY *glances off into the distance and spots the* GYM TEACHER *heading back in their direction.*

They stand up, grind their Sobranies into the mud and set off at a brisk trot. The Sobranie stubs come to rest near a pile of dog poo.

HATTIE, TINA *and* JENNY *are sitting on their desks,*
waiting for a lesson to start. HATTIE *shows* JENNY *a*
piece of paper which apparently contains some kind of
shopping list.

> TINA
>
> (*pointing at Hattie, then at herself*)
> Chanel perfume, Chanel perfume. (*She*
> *repeats the gesture.*) Chanel lipstick, Chanel
> lipstick.
>
> HATTIE
>
> Those funny cigarettes you were smoking.
> Sobranies. Ten packets each.

A very SMALL GIRL, *twelve or thirteen, comes in to the*
classroom and approaches JENNY. *She's clutching a*
ten-shilling note.

> SMALL GIRL
>
> How much is the Chanel perfume?

TINA, HATTIE *and* JENNY *stare at her, nonplussed.*

> Well, are you the girl going to Paris or are
> you not, because . . .

MISS STUBBS *comes into the classroom carrying books*
and essays. She sees the SMALL GIRL *and shoos her out*
while the other girls follow. As JENNY *comes past, she*
whispers discreetly into her ear.

MISS STUBBS

Jenny, the headmistress wants a word with you. The legend of Mr Rochester may have travelled further than you intended.

JENNY *looks at her, startled and a little sick.*

60 INTERIOR: HEADMISTRESS'S OFFICE/CORRIDOR – DAY

The office is dark, wood-panelled, foreboding, apparently designed to put all visitors ill-at-ease. The HEADMISTRESS *would probably choose to be wood-panelled if she could. She's tweedy, bespectacled, severe. There is a knock at the door. She doesn't look up from her paperwork.*

HEADMISTRESS

Come.

JENNY *enters, looking young and frightened.*

Ah. Miss Mellor.

JENNY *tries to look at her with all the courage she can muster.*

We're all very excited about your forthcoming trip to Paris. Our excitement, indeed, knows no bounds. Some of us can talk of little else.

JENNY *looks at her feet.*

An older man, I understand? A word of warning, Miss Mellor. There may well have been the odd sixth-form girl who has lost an important part of herself – perhaps the best part – while under our supervision. These things happen, regrettably. If, however, we are made aware of this loss, then of course the young lady in question would have to continue her studies elsewhere, if, that is, she still has any use for A-levels. Do I make myself clear?

JENNY

Can I go now?

HEADMISTRESS

If you would.

JENNY *turns round and walks out without saying another word.*

61 INTERIOR: JENNY'S HOUSE – EVENING

GRAHAM, JENNY *and her father are at the dinner table, sitting in the dark.*

JACK

(*shouting to* MARJORIE)
What are you doing in there?

JENNY

Well, I imagine she's lighting the candles on my cake.

JACK

You're seventeen, not two hundred and fifty.

There is an awkward pause.

GRAHAM

Thanks for inviting me.

JACK

It was Marjorie's idea, not mine. Not even Jenny's, come to that.

GRAHAM *looks stung.*

JENNY

(*appalled*)
Dad!

MARJORIE *kicks the door open with her foot and comes in holding a birthday cake with seventeen candles burning on it. She puts it down carefully on the table.*

JACK

Blow them out, before the house burns down.

JENNY *closes her eyes, blows out her candles, just as –*

GRAHAM

Make a . . . oh, OK. Don't worry . . .

Everyone applauds as JACK *gets up to turn the lights on. We can see that by* JENNY'S *side is an unopened, carefully wrapped present – clearly a book.*

MARJORIE

Who'd like a piece?

In truth, the cake is a rather sorry and unappetising specimen. There isn't enough icing on the top. She cuts a couple of slices which immediately collapse.

GRAHAM

It doesn't matter . . .

JACK

Come on. Presents.

Without any real enthusiasm, JENNY *opens the present.*

It's a new Latin dictionary.

JENNY

Oh. Thank you. I needed a new one.

GRAHAM

(crestfallen)
Oh dear. Snap!

GRAHAM *hands over a wrapped present exactly the same size and shape as the dictionary.*

The doorbell rings. JACK *goes to answer it, and immediately the house is energised: it's* DAVID.

From the hallway:

JACK *(out of sight)*

Good grief. You should see this!

DAVID *enters. You can hardly see him for all the parcels and flowers he's carrying.*

DAVID

It's a special day.

JENNY, *delighted, moves the dictionaries to make way for* DAVID'S *presents.*

JACK

Makes your dictionary look a bit feeble, eh, Graham?

GRAHAM

Gosh!

GRAHAM *looks pained.* MARJORIE *notices.*

MARJORIE

And ours, too, come to that.

DAVID

And these are for you.

DAVID *gives* MARJORIE *a basket of beautiful roses.*

MARJORIE

Oh, David.

DAVID

(*to* GRAHAM)
Hello, young man.

JACK

David, would you like a drink?

DAVID

I'd love one.

GRAHAM

I'd best be going. I've got a stack of homework to do.

GRAHAM *says his goodbyes.* DAVID *sits down in his
place.*

MARJORIE

Wonderful to see you, Graham.

GRAHAM

(*to* JENNY)
Goodbye, Jenny.

JENNY

(*brightly, without looking up*)
Bye, Graham.

GRAHAM *makes to leave with a last attempt to catch*
JENNY'S *eye, without success.* MARJORIE *shows him to
the door.*

JACK

A little something warming?

DAVID

You know me so well.

Hearty laughter from the two men.

JENNY

Can I open anything yet?

MARJORIE *comes back into the room.*

MARJORIE

Wait for me.

DAVID

Before you open that lot, I've got a surprise.
Next weekend, we're all going to Café de
Flore to celebrate Jenny's birthday.

JACK

(flatly)
Lovely.

DAVID

Café de Flore is in the Boulevard St Ger-
main. In Paris.

JENNY *giggles her delight.* JACK'S *smile is a little more
forced.*

JACK

How d'you mean, Paris?

JENNY

You know the one, Dad.

JACK

(panic rising)

But . . . We don't have any French money.
And besides, it's too . . . I don't think it
would *agree* with me.

JENNY

Dad!

JACK

The French don't like us, Jenny, you know
that. John Sutton from work, he went there
last year. They were very rude to him.

JENNY *understands* DAVID'S *ploy perfectly, and the role
she must play. Her eyes fill with tears.* JACK *notices.*

I don't want to spoil anyone's fun, but . . . It's
just not for me, Europe. You'll have to go
another time.

JENNY

(*bitterly*)
You've just said you don't like Europe. What's
going to change? It'll have to be Europe,
won't it? Because it certainly won't be you.

MARJORIE

I'll take her.

JACK

(*genuinely indignant*)
To the Continent? And leave me here on my
own?

JENNY

Oh, for God's sake.

JENNY *gets up furiously and takes her presents to the other side of the sitting room.*

JACK *looks cornered. He needs to find a way out.*

DAVID

What do you think? You know what Jenny's like about France, Jack. About French films and books and music.

He looks at JACK *for a response.*

JACK
(*discomfited*)
Of course I do.

DAVID

Sorry. Yes. It goes without saying. She's your daughter. Jenny likes to joke about how you're a stick-in-the mud and all the rest of it, but I know that's not who you are. Otherwise she wouldn't be who she is.

JACK
(*uncertainly*)
No.

DAVID

But I can also see that I've acted out of turn, and I'm sorry.

JACK *looks at* JENNY. *Even he can see that he can't do this to her.*

> JACK
>
> What about your Aunt Helen?

DAVID *catches* JENNY'S *eye and she smiles.* JACK *smiles, too; he's off the hook.*

62   EXTERIOR: TWICKENHAM, STREET – NIGHT

The Bristol is speeding down the road.

> JENNY
>
> An hour late.

> DAVID
>
> We'll make it, I promise.

63   INTERIOR: HEATHROW HOTEL BEDROOM – EVENING

DAVID *and* JENNY *enter the room.*

> DAVID
>
> OK, there's a flight at eight in the morning.

> JENNY
>
> Good.

JENNY *stares at the featureless sitting room.*

There's no bed.

DAVID

I pushed the boat out and got us a suite.

JENNY

A suite!

DAVID

If work stops us getting to Paris until tomorrow, then work can buy us a nice hotel room. Anyway, it's a special occasion, isn't it?

JENNY

I'd have thought that tonight of all nights we only need a bed.

Close on DAVID'S *reaction – she hasn't forgotten that tonight's the night.*

64   INTERIOR: HOTEL BEDROOM – NIGHT

DAVID *and* JENNY *in bed, in a dimly lit bedroom. They are kissing –* DAVID *more passionately than* JENNY. *He is making little whimpers of excitement, and* JENNY *is clearly trying hard to hide her nerves. We're acutely aware of her age, and of her virginity. Suddenly* DAVID *breaks off.*

DAVID

Hold on one second. I've got something.

Rather absurdly, he disappears into the other room to look for something. He comes back with a banana. JENNY *stares at him.*

I thought . . . I thought we might want to practice with this.

He brandishes the banana. JENNY *shrieks with horror.*

JENNY

With a banana?

DAVID

I thought we might get the messy bit over with first.

JENNY

David! I don't want to lose my virginity to a piece of fruit.

DAVID

I'm sorry.

DAVID *attempts to kiss her again.* JENNY *wriggles clear.*

JENNY

I think the moment might have gone.
I think we should wait until Paris.

DAVID

I'm an idiot and I'm sorry.

JENNY *doesn't deny it.*

> JENNY
>
> David . . . if tomorrow night does happen, it will only ever happen once.

> DAVID
>
> (*alarmed*)
> Why will it only ever happen once?

> JENNY
>
> Because the first time can only ever happen once.

> DAVID
>
> (*relieved*)
> Oh.

> JENNY
>
> So, no baby-talk. No Minnie. Just treat me like a grown-up.

DAVID *looks chastened.*

> (*brightly*)
> I know. Let's go and sit in our sitting room.

> DAVID
>
> (*cheered up*)
> All right! We'll order up some champagne.

JENNY *looks at him with what might, from one angle, be construed as fondness.*

MONTAGE SEQUENCE – PARIS

Juliette Greco on the soundtrack. DAVID *and* JENNY
take the trip down the Seine past the Eiffel Tower.
They peruse the bookstalls along the river bank.

JENNY *poses with the Seine and Notre Dame behind*
her. DAVID *takes her picture. She looks fantastic in the*
clothes DAVID *has given her for her birthday.*

A handsome Parisian on a moped rides by and eyes up
JENNY, *to* DAVID'S *annoyance.*

DAVID *and* JENNY *dance by the banks of the river.*

They end up at sunset with wine and a picnic looking
out across the Seine.

65   EXTERIOR: PARIS HOTEL – DAWN

JENNY *is smoking on the second-floor balcony of a*
simple, pretty Parisian hotel, wearing a glamorous-
looking slip and looking across at the Sacre Coeur.

66   INTERIOR: HOTEL ROOM – DAWN

The bedroom is simple and romantic – everything the
airport hotel wasn't. DAVID *is lying amid rumpled sheets,*
smoking what is clearly a post-coital cigarette, and
watching JENNY *from behind.*

DAVID

Do you still feel like a schoolgirl?

JENNY *turns and steps in, smiles, shakes her head.*

It wasn't too uncomfortable?

JENNY

Not after the . . . first bit. It's funny, though,
isn't it? All that poetry, and all those songs,
about something that lasts no time at all?

DAVID *looks at her. She isn't being cruel. She just doesn't
know any different. She returns to the view. He smokes
ruminatively.*

67   INTERIOR: CLASSROOM – DAY

JENNY'S *English class, including* HATTIE *and* TINA, *file
past* MISS STUBBS *at the end of a lesson.*

MISS STUBBS

And your exercise books on my desk in a pile,
please.

MISS STUBBS *clearly has something to say to* JENNY,
but is hesitant; JENNY *wants to talk to her, too, but is
equally shy. Eventually* JENNY *produces a bottle of
perfume from her school bag.*

JENNY

I bought this for you.

She holds it out. MISS STUBBS *doesn't take it.*

MISS STUBBS

That's very kind of you, but I can't accept it.

JENNY

Why not?

MISS STUBBS

(*gently*)
It's because of people like you that I plough through illiterate essays by Sandra Lovell about her pony. But I know where this came from, and if I took it, I'd feel I would be betraying both of us.

JENNY *puts the perfume back in her bag and starts to leave, but stops when* MISS STUBBS *speaks again.*

You can do anything you want. You know that. You're clever and you're pretty . . . Is your boyfriend interested in clever Jenny?

JENNY

(*frustrated*)
I'm not quite sure what you're trying to tell me.

MISS STUBBS

I'm telling you to go to Oxford. No matter what. Because if you don't, you'll break my heart.

JENNY *looks at her.*

JENNY

(*quietly*)

Where did you go?

MISS STUBBS

Cambridge.

JENNY

Well, you're clever. And you're pretty. So presumably, Clever Miss Stubbs won. And here you are with your pony essays. I don't know. These last few months, I've eaten in wonderful restaurants and been to jazz clubs and watched wonderful films, heard beautiful music . . .

MISS STUBBS

Jenny, are you taking precautions?

JENNY *stares at her angrily.*

JENNY

It's nothing to do with that.

MISS STUBBS

Isn't it?

JENNY

Maybe all our lives are going to end up with pony essays. Or housework. And yes, maybe we will go to Oxford. But if we're all going to die the moment we graduate, isn't it what we do before that counts?

MISS STUBBS

I'm sorry you think I'm dead.

JENNY

I don't think you're dead, I just don't . . .

MISS STUBBS

(*coldly*)

I think you'd better get to your next class.

JENNY *walks out of the room angrily.*

68 EXTERIOR: DOG TRACKS – NIGHT

A dog-race is coming to its conclusion. DANNY, HELEN,
DAVID *and* JENNY *are watching in the crowd – the girls
jump up and down.* JENNY'S *dog has won.*

HELEN

Well done, Jenny!

JENNY

(*beaming*)

I've never won anything before. Not even at
the Women's Institute raffle.

HELEN

I always bet on the sweetest-looking dog. And
he always comes last.

JENNY

Can we do it again? I'm feeling lucky.

DANNY

Come on, let's go, I don't want to miss him.
Pick up your ten bob on the way out.

JENNY

(*thrilled*)
I won ten shillings?

They start to walk through the crowd.

Who is this man, anyway?

DAVID

Peter Rachman?

DANNY

A complete bastard.

The men laugh.

JENNY

Why do we have to see him here?

DANNY

Because he's not the sort of chap with an
office.

INTERIOR: DOG-TRACK CLUB –
        NIGHT

*They enter a crowded, smoky bar with a dance floor and
a small jukebox.*

*The bar is full of sharply dressed and dubious-looking
men, and young, glamorous, dubious-looking women.*
JENNY *and* HELEN *look out of place –* HELEN *too
ethereal,* JENNY *too innocent.*

*They find a table looking over the race track. A waiter
comes over to their table.*

> DANNY
>
> A bottle of your finest champagne, please.
> (*nodding to the bar*) There he is.

*We see a nasty-looking man in his late thirties/early
forties. He is wearing a white sharkskin suit and smoking
a big cigar. He's talking to an even nastier-looking man
in a dark suit.*

> DAVID
>
> Come on, Jenny. Tell them your good news.
> Don't be bashful.

> HELEN
>
> No. Be Sneezy.

Everyone ignores her.

> DAVID
>
> Jenny got two As and a B in her mock A-levels.

DANNY

(*mock dismissive*)
Like everyone else in this sophisticated establishment.

Laughter.

Seriously, congratulations.

DAVID

The B was in Latin.

Rachman is now standing on his own. DANNY *nudges* DAVID, *and they go over to talk to him just as the champagne arrives. The waiter pops the bottle of champagne and pours two glasses. The girls smile and clink glasses.*

HELEN

Don't worry too much.

JENNY

About what?

HELEN

Someone told me that in fifty years no one will speak Latin, probably. Not even Latin people. So you don't worry about your B.

JENNY *stares at her, trying to think of a response.*

DANNY *and* DAVID *are moving through the bar, having just finished talking to Rachman.* DANNY *puffs out his cheeks and shakes his head.*

DAVID

He's even more of a bastard than I thought.

DANNY

You wouldn't want him to marry your sister. You wouldn't want to talk to him in a club, come to that.

They both chuckle. There is a silence for a moment.

(*gently*)
You do know what you're doing, old chap? With Jenny?

DAVID

This is the one, Danny.

They look over at JENNY *and* HELEN *laughing.*

You can see she's different.

DANNY

I just don't want to see her hurt.

They make their way back to their table.

While DAVID *and* HELEN *watch,* DANNY *and* JENNY
dance. DANNY'S *a good dancer;* JENNY *is nervous at
first, but becomes more comfortable and more expressive,
with* DANNY'S *help.*

> JENNY
>
> (*knowing that she should make conversation, as
> all the couples around her are doing*)
> Have you . . . Have you bought any more
> paintings recently?
>
> DANNY
>
> Have I? Oh yes, I picked up a little Piper. A
> good 'un, I think.
>
> JENNY
>
> I'm still trying to work out what makes good
> things good. It's hard, isn't it?
>
> DANNY
>
> The thing is, Jenny, you know, without neces-
> sarily being able to explain why. You've got
> taste. That's not even half the battle. That's
> the whole war.

JENNY *smiles at him with gratitude. There is a sudden
closeness between them.* DAVID *is watching them carefully. They return to their table.*

DAVID

Jenny, we should go. It's late.

JENNY

(*disappointed*)
Really?

DANNY

Alas. One day, school will be over forever,
and we can talk about art all night.

DAVID

(*to Danny*)
You're all right in a taxi, aren't you?

He guides JENNY *firmly out of the club.*

72   EXTERIOR: CLUB – NIGHT

JENNY *is about to to open the passenger door of the
Bristol, but* DAVID *stops her.*

DAVID

Wait here.

*He runs to the back of the car, opens the boot and starts
rummaging through it. It seems to be full of everything
but the thing he's looking for.*

JENNY

What are you looking for? . . . What are you
doing?

He comes back empty-handed.

DAVID

Will you marry me?

JENNY *stares at him for a moment, then laughs.*

JENNY

What were you looking for?

DAVID

I thought I had a ring. It wouldn't have been
the right one. But it would have done for
tonight.

JENNY

(*eyes twinkling with amusement*)
Oh, David.

DAVID

I'm serious.

JENNY

You're very sweet.

DAVID

What do you think?

JENNY

(*helplessly*)
Take me home.

She gets into the car. We see the desperation in DAVID'S *face, lit by the headlights of a passing taxi, as he slams the door on* JENNY *after she's got in.*

73   INTERIOR: JENNY'S BEDROOM

JENNY *is at her desk in her bedroom, trying to work, but she can't concentrate. Her hair is tied back in a ponytail. She gets up, pulls back the curtains, looks out of the window, smoking. We see what she sees: a sleepy suburban street at night; a couple walking away in the distance. She looks back at her desk. It looks even more boring than the street.*

74   INTERIOR: JENNY'S KITCHEN – EVENING

JENNY'S *mother and father are doing the washing-up and listening to the radio. They have their backs to the door.* JENNY *enters the room quietly and watches them for a moment.*

> MAN ON THE RADIO
> They do need some looking after, but nothing that will require too much work. Just leave them in your potting shed for a couple of weeks, and they'll look after themselves.

JACK

Fine, the potting shed. Who does he think I
am? Prince Rainier of Monaco?

JENNY

What if I got married instead of going to
college?

JACK *and* MARJORIE *turn around.*

JACK

Married?

JENNY

Married.

JACK

It would depend who it was, surely?

JENNY

Would it? That's interesting.

JACK

Well, of course it would. I wouldn't want you
married off just for the sake of it.

JENNY

Thanks.

MARJORIE

Has somebody asked you?

JENNY

Yes.

JACK

Who?

MARJORIE *rolls her eyes.*

David?

JENNY

No. A man I just met walking his dog.

MARJORIE

What did you tell him?

JENNY

Nothing yet.

MARJORIE

Do you have a choice? Or is it too late?

She looks at her daughter knowingly. JACK *merely looks confused.*

JACK

Of course she's got a choice! An interesting one, too, eh?

JENNY

This is where you're supposed to say, 'But what about Oxford?'

JACK

Look at it another way, you wouldn't really
need to go now, would you?

JENNY

(*quietly, turning the words over in her mouth*)
I wouldn't need to go. Would you like to
expand on that?

JACK

You'd be looked after.

JENNY *laughs bitterly. She can't believe it.*

JENNY

All that Latin! All those essays! What was the
point? Why didn't you just send me out prowl-
ing round nightclubs? It would have been less
trouble. And I might have had more fun.

JACK

I don't know about nightclubs. I know about
education. Anyway, looks like it might have
all turned out for the best.

JENNY

How?

JACK

He wouldn't want you if you were thick, now
would he?

JENNY *stares at them.*

English. MISS STUBBS *is standing at the front of the class, holding a copy of* King Lear, *and listening as various members of the class massacre the text. Some are messing about by overacting; others read to the best of their ability, tonelessly and with no understanding of the words.*

Lear himself is being read by ANN, *the bespectacled girl from the first scene. She's no King Lear, and she's one of the bad readers.*

> GIRL
>
> May not an ass know when the cart draws the horse? Sings whoop jug I love thee.

> MISS STUBBS
>
> When it says 'sings', it means you should sing the line.

GIRL *looks at her blankly.*

> Never mind. Right. (*gesturing to* ANN)
> Lear . . .

> ANN
>
> Does any here know me. This is not Lear. Does Lear walk thus?

> TINA
>
> (*sotto voce, to* JENNY, *in the seat next to her*)
> No.

JENNY *starts to giggle.*

ANN

Speak thus?

TINA *shakes her head.*

Where are his eyes?

TINA *doesn't need to say anything – she just looks at* JENNY, *makes a pair of spectacles with her fingers and squints.*

JENNY'S *giggling fit increases in intensity.*

Ha! Waking? Who is it that can tell me who I am?

JENNY'S *arm shoots up, as if to answer the question.*

JENNY

Ooh. Miss. Me. I can.

MISS STUBBS *looks at* JENNY *more in sorrow than in anger –* JENNY'S *behaviour now is something new in their relationship.* JENNY *stares back at her defiantly. Suddenly* MISS STUBBS *notices something glinting on her hand: an engagement ring.*

MISS STUBBS

Oh, Jenny.

She is, as she promised she would be, heartbroken.

JENNY

What?

MISS STUBBS

Take it off.

HATTIE, *who is sitting behind* JENNY, *notices the ring, too, for the first time.*

> HATTIE
>
> Oh my God. Is that what I think it is? I'M GOING TO BE A BRIDESMAID!

There is an excited susurration in the classroom.

> MISS STUBBS
>
> You know the school rule on jewellery.

> JENNY
>
> Half the girls in this room are wearing jewellery.

> MISS STUBBS
>
> Yes. But none of it is going to ruin their lives.

> JENNY
>
> (*coolly*)
> We have a difference of opinion about that.

MISS STUBBS *stares at her.* JENNY *can only just steel herself to stare back.*

76 INTERIOR: HEADMISTRESS'S OFFICE – DAY

> HEADMISTRESS
>
> How far advanced are these ridiculous plans?

Have you set a date? Have you decided on a church?

JENNY

We won't be getting married in a church. David's Jewish.

The HEADMISTRESS *stares at her, dumbfounded.*

HEADMISTRESS

Jewish? He's a Jew? You're aware, I take it, that the Jews killed our Lord?

JENNY

(*beginning to feel less intimidated by her surroundings*)
And you're aware, I suppose, that our Lord was Jewish?

The HEADMISTRESS *snorts scornfully.*

HEADMISTRESS

I suppose *he* told you that. We're all very sorry about what happened during the war. But that's absolutely no excuse for that sort of malicious and untruthful propaganda.

JENNY *smiles to herself.*

Anyway, I can see you're far more in need of responsible advice than I realised.

The HEADMISTRESS *moves closer.*

Nobody does anything worth doing without a degree.

JENNY

Nobody does anything worth doing with a degree. No woman, anyway.

HEADMISTRESS

So what I do isn't worth doing? Or what Miss Stubbs does, or Mrs Wilson, or any of us here?

JENNY *doesn't say anything. The headmistress takes her silence as an admission of defeat.*

Because none of us would be here without our degrees, you realise that, don't you? And yes, of course studying is hard, and boring, and . . .

JENNY *can't contain herself any longer.*

JENNY

Boring!

HEADMISTRESS

I'm sorry?

JENNY

Studying is hard and boring. Teaching is hard and boring. So what you're telling me is to be bored, and then bored, and then finally bored again, but this time for the rest of my life. This whole stupid country is bored. There's no life in it, or colour, or fun. It's probably just as well that the Russians are going to

drop a nuclear bomb on us any day now. So
my choice is to do something hard and boring, *or* to marry my . . . my *Jew* and go to
Paris and Rome and listen to jazz and read
and eat good food in nice restaurants and
have fun. It's not enough to educate us any
more, Miss Walters. You've got to tell us why
you're doing it.

She has never had to answer this questions before.

HEADMISTRESS

It doesn't have to be teaching, you know.
There's the Civil Service.

JENNY

I don't wish to be impertinent, Miss Walters.
But it is an argument worth rehearsing. You
never know. Someone else might want to
know the point of it all, one day.

JENNY *leaves the office.*

77   EXTERIOR: SCHOOL – DAY

JENNY *is half-walking, half-running, towards the school
gates. She's scared, of course, but exhilarated, too. All that
pressure, and all those years of education, suddenly over,
unexpectedly, and certainly unceremoniously. She looks
neither left nor right, but other girls, younger girls, watch
her through the windows as she leaves.* JENNY *doesn't
even look round when she goes through the school gates.*

DANNY, HELEN, DAVID *and* JENNY *are in* DANNY'S
flat. DANNY *has a large stuffed armadillo on his lap,
which he is using as a ventriloquist's dummy. The armadillo is at his ear, and* DANNY *makes a squeaking sound.
The others are laughing.*

>   DANNY
>
>   (*to* JENNY)
>   I think he likes you. Do you like her? . . . Yes,
>   I do like her. You don't remember? It's Jenny.
>   You remember her from last time. No, I
>   don't . . . Yes, you do. Naughty thing . . .
>   Pardon? . . . That's revolting! You stick to
>   your own species. (*whispers*) He wants to
>   kiss you, I think. Is that naughty?

>   DAVID
>
>   (*suddenly, out of nowhere*)
>   We're engaged.

The atmosphere changes. JENNY *looks embarrassed.*
HELEN *and* DANNY *look at her, and she holds up her ring.*

>   HELEN
>
>   That's . . . Gosh. That's fantastic news.

>   JENNY
>
>   Thank you.

DANNY *isn't so pleased.*

DANNY
(*cool*)
Congratulations.

There is much chinking of glasses.

HELEN
I knew you'd see sense about university.

JENNY *smiles.*

You'll stay pretty now.

Laughter from DAVID *and* JENNY.

JENNY
Can I still read?

HELEN
(*firmly*)
Yes, but it doesn't have to be books, now
does it? Magazines will do just as well. And
you learn more from them anyway.

Laughter.

DAVID
Oh, Helen.

HELEN
You won't be laughing, David, when she goes
all speccy and spotty.

HELEN *is bemused by their mirth.* DANNY *watches*
DAVID *thoughtfully.*

79   EXTERIOR: DANNY'S FLAT – NIGHT

DAVID *and* JENNY *come out of* DANNY'S *flat and approach* DAVID'S *car.*

> JENNY
>
> Danny didn't seem very pleased about our engagement.

> DAVID
>
> I noticed that, too. I thought he might be a bit jealous.

> JENNY
>
> (*trying not to be pleased*)
> Jealous?

> DAVID
>
> We're going to keep him away from you.

They both smile. DAVID *opens the door for* JENNY *and she gets into the car.*

80   INTERIOR: JENNY'S HOUSE – EVENING

JENNY *and* MARJORIE *are in the hall, all dressed up and waiting for* DAVID *to come and pick them up.* JENNY *looks great, as usual; her mother looks smart, if somewhat old-fashioned.*

JACK *comes in from the sitting room, pulling at his tie,*

looking apprehensive. He appears to be wearing Bryl-
creem. He looks like a little boy who has been made to
put on his Sunday best.

JACK

I mean, what is one supposed to order as a
starter, anyway? And how will I know what is
a starter and what isn't?

JENNY

We've been through this, Dad. It'll be quite
clearly marked on the menu.

The doorbell rings. JACK *stiffens.* JENNY *goes to answer*
the door.

JACK

Can't the three of you go on your own and
leave me here? I'd be perfectly happy with a
tin of salmon.

DAVID *enters the room. He is relaxed, happy. He has*
worn a tie, possibly because he knew that JACK *would*
wear a tie. JACK *and* MARJORIE *exchange greetings.*

DAVID

Ready? I think you'll like this place, Jack.
Their wine list is as good as anything I've
seen in London.

JACK

Yes, someone told me that.

JENNY

David, probably. Who else would it have
been?

81   EXTERIOR: STREET/JENNY'S HOUSE –
      NIGHT

JACK *and* MARJORIE *approach* DAVID'S *Bristol.*

DAVID

(*holding the door for* MARJORIE)
Madame.

JACK

I was hoping you'd take us in this.

DAVID

Oh, you won't want to drive in anything else
after tonight. Mind you, it drinks petrol. I'm
afraid we'll have to stop on the way in to
town.

He opens the back door for his future father-in-law.

82   EXTERIOR: DAVID'S CAR – NIGHT

The Bristol drives away down JENNY'S *street.*

JACK

I feel like Eamonn Andrews.

DAVID

Is that a good thing?

MARJORIE

Eamonn Andrews is the poshest person that
Jack can imagine being.

Everyone laughs.

83 INTERIOR/EXTERIOR: DAVID'S CAR/ STREET – NIGHT

The Bristol cruises down a London road.

84 EXTERIOR: PETROL STATION – NIGHT

The Bristol pulls into the garage. DAVID *gets out of the
car as the attendant comes over.*

ATTENDANT

How are you tonight, sir?

DAVID

Very well. Might as well fill her up.

DAVID *leans in through the open car window.*

I'm just going to make a quick call. I'll be
two ticks.

INTERIOR/EXTERIOR: DAVID'S CAR/
PETROL STATION – NIGHT

JENNY *watches him walk towards the garage office.*

> JACK
>
> Do you think I should offer to help pay for
> the petrol? Would he be insulted, do you
> think?

JENNY *watches* DAVID *as he picks up the phone. He
notices her and waves from behind the glass.*

> I know he said tonight was his treat, but does
> that apply to the petrol, do you think?

> MARJORIE
>
> I'm sure it does, Jack.

They lapse into silence. JACK *starts to fiddle with the
features in the car – a piece of the window handle snaps
off in* JACK'S *hand, much to his alarm.*

> JACK
>
> Oh, no.

> MARJORIE
>
> Jack!

> JACK
>
> It just came off.

JENNY *opens the glove compartment, looking for the
cigarettes that* DAVID *always keeps there. She finds the*

cigarettes and closes the glove compartment. But she has seen something in there, so she opens it again. She takes out some letters and papers and starts to look through them.

86 EXTERIOR: PETROL STATION – NIGHT

DAVID *has finished his phone call and is walking towards the car.*

> DAVID
> (*to attendant*)
> Put it on my bill.

> ATTENDANT
> Thank you, sir.

He sees JENNY *looking through letters and papers, sees the open glove compartment and leans in through the passenger window.*

> DAVID
> (*desperately*)
> Jenny!

It's too late. We see JENNY'S *stricken face, gleaming in someone else's headlights.*

87 INTERIOR/EXTERIOR: DAVID'S CAR/ PETROL STATION – NIGHT

DAVID *gets into the car.*

> DAVID
> Jenny, I . . .

> JENNY
> (*as cold as ice*)
> Take us home.

> JACK
> What's wrong?

> DAVID
> I'm afraid there's been . . . Jenny's had a bit of a shock.

> JACK
> What's happened?

> JENNY
> It's just another one of David's little muddles and misunderstandings.

> DAVID
> I . . .

> JENNY
> I don't want to hear another word from anybody. Take us home. NOW.

MARJORIE *and* JACK *look at each other.* DAVID *swings the car round and they drive home in silence.*

88   EXTERIOR: JENNY'S HOUSE – NIGHT

The Bristol draws up outside JENNY'S *house. Everyone gets out of the car.* JACK *starts to walk towards the house and then stops.*

> JACK
>
> (*desperately*)
> You can take care of this, can't you, David?
>
> JENNY
>
> Go inside, Dad.

JENNY *and* DAVID *watch* JACK *and* MARJORIE *go into the house. The moment the door is closed,* JENNY *turns towards* DAVID. *She's holding a bunch of letters that she took out of the glove compartment. She starts to go through them, one by one.*

> Mr and Mrs David Goldman, Mr and Mrs David Goldman, Mr and Mrs David Goldman . . . (*thrusting an envelope angrily at him*)
> You're MARRIED!
>
> DAVID
>
> Legally, yes, but . . .

JENNY *is distraught and tearful.*

JENNY

When were you going to tell me?

DAVID

Soon. It just never seemed like the right
time. You seemed so happy, and I was
happy . . .

JENNY

You were living with your wife all this time
. . . round the corner. Byron Avenue! It's no
wonder we kept bumping into each other,
then, is it? What number?

DAVID

Thirty-four.

JENNY *picks out one of the envelopes and looks at it, as if
to check he's not lying again.*

Don't be like this. Come on.

JENNY

I have nothing. I didn't take my exams. I – I
left school. Where's it all gone, now?

DAVID

I can get a divorce. Everything will turn out
for the best.

We can see JACK *and* MARJORIE *peering through the
lace curtains anxiously.*

JENNY

Go and tell them. Go and tell them, then go
and tell your wife.

DAVID *stands on the pavement, looking towards the
house.*

DAVID

They won't listen now. I'll come round tomorrow. When everyone's feeling a bit calmer.

JENNY

(*suddenly desperate*)
Please don't make me . . . Please don't make
me tell them on my own. You owe me that
much. You owe them that much.

DAVID

(*sadly*)
I owe them much more than that.

He opens the boot. It's full of cases of whisky. JENNY
doesn't even bother asking what they are doing there.
DAVID *takes one of the bottles.*

JENNY

Two minutes. And then I'll come out and
drag you in.

JENNY *marches into the house and slams the door. The
camera stays on* DAVID. *He gets back into the car, opens
the bottle and takes a slug of whisky. Then his shoulders
begin to shake, and he starts to cry.*

JENNY s*tands in the hall, waiting, tears in her eyes. She walks into the sitting room. Her parents are sitting on the sofa looking at her anxiously. They haven't put the lights on yet.*

> JACK
>
> What's going on?

> JENNY
>
> He's helping himself to some Dutch courage before facing you. Stolen Dutch courage, from the look of it. He has something to tell you.

She sits down, pale and young-looking again, opposite her parents. Suddenly they are all three lit up by head-lights. Shot from their point-of-view of the Bristol roaring off up the street.

> JACK
>
> He just drove off.

We close slowly in on JENNY'S *face. But of course he'd drive off!*

> (*pathetic*)
> Can you tell us? Jenny, please?

JENNY *can't deal with her own pain, let alone his. He already looks like a broken, foolish old man. They should hug. But they don't.*

JENNY *is sitting on the sofa in* DANNY'S *flat.* DANNY *is in his dressing gown; there are newspapers strewn around.* HELEN *is sitting next to her, holding her hand.*

HELEN

I wouldn't worry about it too much. When I found out that . . .

DANNY

Not now, Helen.

HELEN *shrugs and goes to get a drink.*

I tried to tell him. I'm not speaking to him now, if that's any consolation.

JENNY

(*bitterly*)
It's a funny world you people live in. You both watched me . . . *carrying on* with a married man, but you didn't think it was worth saying anything about it.

DANNY

Yes, well, if you want that conversation . . . You watched David and I help ourselves to a map, and you didn't say much, either.

He holds JENNY'S *gaze,* HELEN *joins him.* JENNY *looks down.*

*A suburban street, full of semi-detached houses, not far
from* JENNY'S *house.* JENNY *walks down the road tentatively – she's looking at the numbers on the houses. She
looks young again – tired, no make-up, no elegant
clothes. She can't bring herself to wear anything that*
DAVID *bought her.*

   *She hesitates at the gate to the house, steels herself to
walk up the path. But just at that moment the door
opens; there's a homely-looking woman, early thirties*
(SARAH). *She is holding the hand of a four-year-old.*
JENNY *is stunned. The woman holds the boy's hand as
they walk away from the house, then she stops in her
tracks.*

> SARAH
> Oh. Hello.

> JENNY
> (*almost inaudible*)
> Hello. Sorry. I think I must have the wrong
> number.

The woman stares at her.

> I was looking for my . . . cello lesson. I
> wanted . . .

She dries up and looks at the woman helplessly.

SARAH

Oh, no. Don't tell me. Good God. You're a *child*.

JENNY *blushes. Beat.*

You didn't know about any of this. Presumably?

JENNY *shakes her head.*

No. They never do. You're not in the family way, are you? Because that's happened before.

JENNY *shakes her head.*

Thank God for that.

JENNY *turns and walks away from the house.*

(*calling after her*)
No, no. You stay here.

But JENNY *heads off down the street.*

92   INTERIOR: JENNY'S HOUSE – DAY

MARJORIE *and* JACK *are in the kitchen.* MARJORIE *is smoking. Normal life has clearly been suspended during this crisis.* JENNY *comes in the front door and they both rush to the hallway.*

MARJORIE

Did you see her?

JENNY

Yes, I saw her. I didn't talk to her. There wasn't any need.

JACK

We have to have this out. Well, if you won't do it, I will. I'm still your father.

He grabs his coat.

JENNY

You're my father again, are you? What were you when you encouraged me to throw my life away? Silly schoolgirls are always getting seduced by glamorous older men. But what about you two?

JENNY, *exasperated, disappears upstairs, leaving* JACK *and* MARJORIE *not knowing what to say.*

JACK *storms into the sitting room and slams the door, leaving* MARJORIE *alone in the hall.*

93 INTERIOR: UPPER HALLWAY – NIGHT

JACK *stands outside* JENNY'S *bedroom door with a cup of tea. He knocks tentatively.*

94 INTERIOR: JENNY'S BEDROOM – NIGHT

Close-up of the floaty print dress that HELEN *gave her. The dress is suddenly jerked out of shot, and we pull back to reveal a weeping* JENNY *stuffing it into an already full box of things she is throwing out. The contents represent her now-despised,* DAVID-*created adult self. We can see Juliette Greco albums, photos, expensive-looking jewellery boxes. She continues to stuff things into the box. There's a knock on the door.*

> JACK (*out of sight*)
> Jenny.

She continues to put her DAVID-*life away into bags. She ignores him.*

95 INTERIOR: UPPER HALLWAY – NIGHT

JACK *is almost in tears.*

> JACK
> Jenny. I'm sorry.

No answer.

> I know I've made a mess of everything.

He waits for an answer – nothing.

> All my life I've been scared, and I didn't want
> you to be scared. That's why I wanted you to
> go to Oxford. And then along came David,

and he knew famous writers, he knew how to get to classical music concerts. But he wasn't who he said he was. He wasn't who you said he was, either.

96 INTERIOR: JENNY'S BEDROOM – NIGHT

JENNY *is sitting on the bed, a tear rolls down her cheek and she closes her eyes.*

97 INTERIOR: UPPER HALLWAY – NIGHT

JACK

The other day, your mother and I were listening to a programme about C. S. Lewis on the radio, and they said he'd moved to Cambridge in 1954. I said, Well, they've got that wrong. Our Jenny wouldn't have his name in her book . . . if he'd moved to Cambridge.

98 INTERIOR: JENNY'S BEDROOM – NIGHT

JENNY'S *face crumples. She knows he's right.*

99 INTERIOR: UPPER HALLWAY – NIGHT

JACK

There's a cup of tea and some biscuits out here.

He puts them down on the floor outside her door.

100 INTERIOR: JENNY'S BEDROOM – NIGHT

JENNY *puts her head in her hands and sobs.*

101 INTERIOR: HEADMISTRESS'S OFFICE – DAY

JENNY *has dressed soberly in clothes not unlike a school uniform for this meeting: it completes a circle. She's back where she started from, or would like to be, anyway. If she seems older than she did when we first met her, it's because things have happened to her, and they've left a mark on her face. She's worried and tired. The* HEAD-MISTRESS, *meanwhile, is delighted by her return – but only because of the opportunities for smugness and schadenfreude it provides.*

HEADMISTRESS

How do you think we can help?

JENNY

I want to repeat my last year at school and take my exams.

HEADMISTRESS

I got the impression the last time we spoke that you didn't see the point of school. Or of me, or of any of us here.

JENNY

I know. I was stupid . . . The life I want – there's no shortcut. I know now that I need to go to university.

HEADMISTRESS

It gives me absolutely no pleasure whatsoever to see our schoolgirls throw their lives away. Although, of course, you are not one of our schoolgirls any more. Through your own volition.

JENNY

I suppose you think I'm a ruined woman.

HEADMISTRESS

You're not a woman.

Beat. The HEADMISTRESS *is pleased with her line.*

No, I'm afraid I think that the offer of a place at this school would be wasted on you.

102 INTERIOR: BUS – DUSK

JENNY *looking dejected. The bell goes and she suddenly gets up and heads off the bus.*

103 INTERIOR: MISS STUBBS'S FLAT – DUSK.

It's a proper Bohemian flat. There are books and papers and pictures covering every available surface. JENNY *looks around. Finally, for the first time, we see her in somewhere she can feel at home.*

> MISS STUBBS
> Come in. I didn't expect to see you again.

JENNY *looks around.*

> JENNY
> This is lovely.

MISS STUBBS *makes a face.*

> All your books and pictures and . . .

> MISS STUBBS
> Paperbacks and postcards, Jenny.

> JENNY
> (*apparently understanding something*)
> That's all you need, isn't it? Just somewhere to . . . I'm sorry I said those silly things. I didn't understand.

MISS STUBBS

Let's forget about it.

A postcard catches JENNY'S *eye.*

JENNY

A Burne-Jones.

MISS STUBBS

Do you like him?

JENNY *pauses.*

JENNY

I do. Still.

MISS STUBBS

Still? Gosh, you sound very old and wise.

JENNY

(*heartfelt*)
I feel old. But not very wise. Miss Stubbs . . .
I need your help.

MISS STUBBS

I was so hoping that's what you were going to
say.

MONTAGE SEQUENCE

JENNY *works hard, studying for her exams, the seasons pass . . .*

104 INTERIOR: JENNY'S HOUSE, KITCHEN/HALLWAY – DAY

JENNY, JACK *and* MARJORIE *are finishing breakfast.* JACK *gets up and puts his raincoat on.*

> JACK
>
> Thank you, Marjorie.

He goes into the hallway. JENNY, *still in her pyjamas, hardly looks up from her Penguin book.* JACK *returns to the kitchen with a letter.*

> It's from Oxford.

JENNY *takes the letter, opens it, doesn't give anything away, puts the letter on the table, gets up and goes into the hallway, closing the door to the kitchen.* JACK *nervously hands the letter to* MARJORIE.

> MARJORIE
>
> (*reading*)
>
> 'It is my pleasure to inform you that your application to read English at Oxford has been accepted . . .'

In the hallway, we track in on JENNY, *sitting at the bottom of the stairs, as she smiles.*

Eighteen months later. Swelling orchestral music. Wide shot of Oxford spires. Close on JENNY *cycling, absorbed, happy. The camera pulls back to show her cycling through the streets of Oxford – a male student is cycling with her.*

> JENNY (*voice over*)
>
> So, I went to read English books, and did my best to avoid the speccy, spotty fate that Helen had predicted for me. I probably looked as wide-eyed, fresh and artless as any other student . . . But I wasn't. One of the boys I went out with, and they really were boys, once asked me to go to Paris with him. And I told him I'd love to, I was dying to see Paris . . . as if I'd never been.

JENNY *and her friend cycle away into the distance.*

APPENDIX: ALTERNATIVE ENDING

105   EXTERIOR: STREET IN OXFORD – DAY

Eighteen months later. Swelling orchestral music. Close on JENNY *cycling, absorbed, happy, the cello strapped to her precariously. The camera pulls back to show her cycling through the streets of Oxford – a male student is cycling with her. She's done it. We follow her for a little while. She dismounts outside a church and leans the bike against a wall. Just as she's about to leave it, she sees something and freezes. We follow her gaze: it's the red Bristol, parked a little way down the road just in front of her. She scans the street to see if she can find* DAVID. *She can – he's coming round a corner, a little further down the street, unwrapping a packet of cigarettes.* JENNY *moves into his eye-line. He sees her, stops, then walks towards her.*

JENNY
Good God.

DAVID
Hello, Jenny.

JENNY

What are you doing here?

DAVID

I came to see you.

JENNY

I think in this case, better never than late.

DAVID

Please don't be unkind. And you probably know that I've . . . Been away, so I couldn't come before.

JENNY

Yes. My mother sent me the cutting from the local paper. 'He asked for one hundred and ninety other offences to be taken into consideration.' A hundred and ninety! You must have 'liberated' most of the antiques in the Home Counties.

DAVID

I wanted to make a clean start. For a new life together. I came to tell you that I'm going to ask my wife for a divorce.

JENNY *laughs mirthlessly and disbelievingly.*

JENNY

Don't you understand what you did?

DAVID

Jenny . . . I can see my behaviour must have been . . . confusing. But we've never sat down and had a proper chat about it all. About the whys and wherefores. They can wait. The important thing is that you're still my Minnie Mouse, and I love you, and you had fun. You know you had fun.

JENNY

Yes. I had fun. But I had fun with the wrong person, at all the wrong times. And I can't ever get those times back, now. It was as if I got lost, and ended up in the middle of somebody else's life. But I've got my own life back now. (*beat*) Look, David. I'm in Oxford.

She looks at him and shakes her head, as if awaking from a dream. The student stops behind her on his bike, dismounts, leans his bike against the wall next to hers, waits for her to finish. She turns her back on DAVID, *and the young man offers her his arm. They walk away together, and* DAVID *stares longingly after them.*